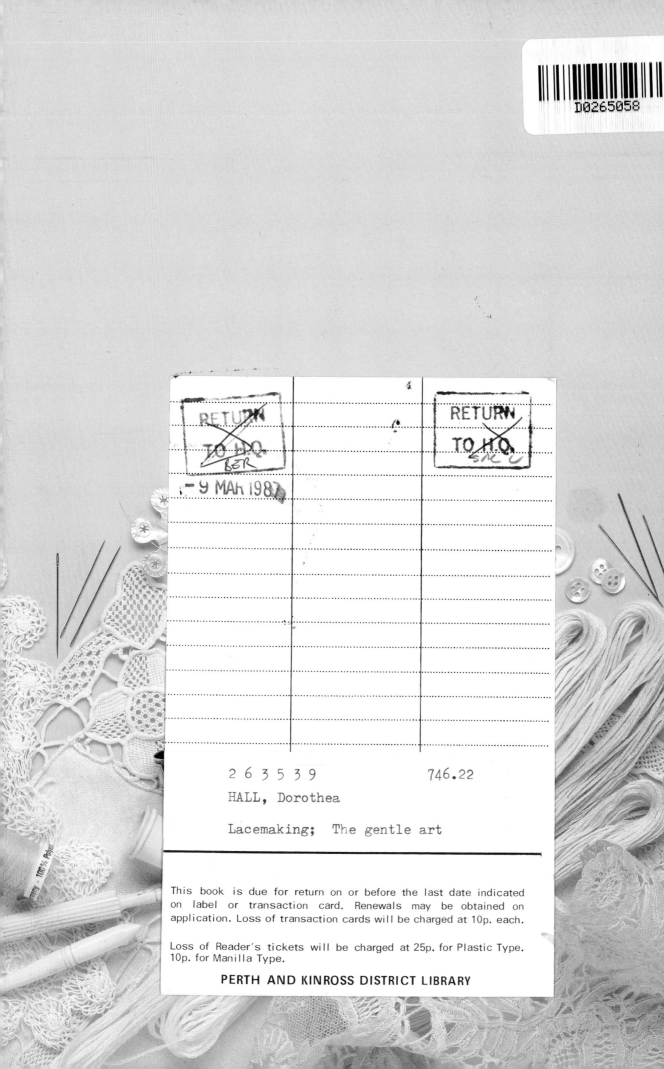

Lacemaking
THE GENTLE ART

WINDWARD

Editor: Dorothea Hall
Art Editor: Caroline Dewing
Designer: Sue Rose
Production: Richard Churchill

Published by Windward,
an imprint owned by W.H. Smith & Sons Limited
Registered No. 237811 England
Trading as WHS Distributors,
St. John's House, East Street, Leicester LE1 6NE

© Marshall Cavendish Limited 1986

ISBN 0 7112 0439 X

Phototypeset by Quadraset Ltd, Midsomer Norton, Avon
Printed and bound in Spain by Jerez Industrial, S.A.

Contents

Foreword

The exact origins of lace are difficult to pinpoint, but it seems probable that it evolved from a mélange of embroidery (needlepoint), network (lacis) and weaving (bobbin lace). Despite the discovery of some form of mesh network in Egyptian tombs, lace as we know it developed from the fine pulled and drawn thread work, cutwork, and darned netting of Mediaeval Europe, emerging in the sixteenth century to remain a delicate and precise craft peculiar to Europe.

In the sixteenth and seventeenth centuries Italy was the main producer of needlepoint laces, while the centres for bobbin lace were Flanders in the North and Spain in the South, where a strong Jewish community specialized in making silver and gold lace.

Bobbin lace found its way to England probably through persecuted Protestants fleeing from Northern Europe. Here lacemaking became a cottage industry, with home workers selling their lace to travelling dealers, but this industry was much affected, firstly by the importing of both needlepoint and bobbin lace from Europe, and later in the eighteenth century by machines that proved to be quicker and cheaper. Attempts were made to halt the flow of foreign lace through taxes and laws, but this only had the effect of making lace more desirable for the rich and fashionable, and thus more lucrative for the smuggler. Smuggling was rife, especially across the Channel and between France and Flanders. It was not unknown for lace to be smuggled into the country in a coffin. Sometimes all that remained of the deceased was the head, feet and hands, the 'body' being lace!

Traditionally, lace was made from linen thread and, later, from silk and cotton in both black and natural colours. These days many types of thread are used, depending on the type of lace being made, ranging from very fine cotton (for Honiton Lace) to heavier wool for more experimental techniques.

Lacemaking takes you through several types of lace — needle lace, bobbin lace, tatting, knitting and crochet — and offers a varied selection of both traditional and contemporary patterns — many of the projects happily combining authentic stitches and techniques in different ways to create interesting new looks.

With lacemaking currently becoming so popular throughout the world, several Guilds and Societies have been formed to further the craft, and in England the Lace Guild was formed in 1976 to assist and encourage the growing interest in all aspects of lace making. 'Lace' is the Lace Guild's quarterly newsletter which, amongst other things contains articles and patterns on the craft to encourage beginners and to provide interest for the more experienced lacemaker. 'Lace' includes details of courses, lace days, classes and lists suppliers of lace requisites. To cater for the increasing number of young people interested in lace making, The Young Lacemakers' Club for under 18s was formed, and they too have their own publication.

In America there are several societies, and probably the most well-known is the International Old Lacers Inc., whose membership extends worldwide. They send out a newsletter every year, and hold an annual convention. There are similar societies in many other countries, for example Canada, Australia, Holland and France. There is also a society for tatters, called the Ring of Tatters, which holds meetings, tatting days, and sends out a regular newsletter.

In conclusion, having read *Lacemaking*, I think it will be a very useful and important addition to the list of craft books available, and it will be indispensable to anyone wishing to take up these lacemaking crafts.

Helen Cavanagh
THE LACE GUILD

Introduction

Such are the vagaries of fashion, that in the past handmade laces have been so highly prized they could be offered as a king's ransom, while at other times discarded as being totally worthless. For example, from the early seventeenth century it is known that Charles I spent at least £1,500 on his personal lace and linen, paying as much as £30 for a pair of shoe roses in metal lace.

Later on, particularly when fashion became utterly simple, notably with Oliver Cromwell and after the French Revolution, and more recently in the 1930s and 40s, great collections of priceless lace were disposed of or destroyed. In Revolutionary France, to be associated with the aristocracy (and the wearing of fine lace) meant death by guillotine, and in the latter case, during the War years, dealers were not sufficiently interested and collectors were few, so that old lace that had been kept in store had no market value.

Today, however, like many other handmade textiles, lace is being rediscovered and revalued for its sheer beauty and skill. To cater for this growing interest in antique textiles, dealers and certain television programmes have done much to promote the current craze for identifying and collecting old lace. As a result there are many people now who are eager to learn more about the different types of lace and how they are made.

The story of lace is told in *Lacemaking* in such a way that even a newcomer to handcrafts can easily learn the fascinating traditional skills and techniques of handmade lace, while making contemporary designs. Nothing is left to chance — each pattern is clearly written and further bolstered, either by step-by-step photographs or by detailed drawings where needed.

The book is divided into six chapters: needle lace; bobbin lace; tatting; knitted lace; crocheted lace; and filet lace, and each one is packed with attractive projects. Some of them, such as the knitted and crocheted edgings, can be made in next to no time, adding an instant touch of prettiness to an otherwise plain edge. Other projects, such as the bobbin lace mat on page 48 and the tatted table centre (page 63) are the culmination of a series of lessons, and will take a little longer to make but the results are truly impressive. There are fashion items and home furnishing projects which will appeal to and inspire both the beginner and more experienced lacemaker — projects with a timeless beauty you'll treasure forever.

Chapter 1

Needle Lace

The term 'needle lace' covers the wide and fascinating variety of lace made entirely with an embroidery needle. It can produce the heavily embossed textures of Venetian needlepoint and the delicacy of Tenerife lace. We've included our tape lace project here since hand-worked bars and buttonhole stitches are used to link the narrow bobbin lace into a typically flowing design.

Needle lace often gives the impression of being extremely complicated but in fact, the basic skills are very easy to learn. These mainly involve working variations of detached buttonhole stitch, simple weaving and knotting stitches.

A beginner could start with the Tenerife lace collar — to accentuate the neck of a plain sweater or dress (see page 24), and progress through the elegant tape lace camisole and the needlepoint picture, learning the traditional skills and stitches that give needle lace its delightful and intricate effects, while applying them in a contemporary way.

Landscape picture

This exquisitely stitched landscape looking on to distant snow-covered mountains is cleverly viewed through an arched window. Reflecting yellow sandstone, its hessian frame is freely embroidered with trailing wall plants.

Materials

Many ordinary sewing silks and machine threads, including mercerized cottons, stranded embroidery thread, *coton à broder* and fine crochet cottons can all be used for working lacy needlepoint stitches. Two different thicknesses of thread are needed to work the embroidery where a fine thread is used for the filing stitch and a heavier thread called a cordonnet for the outline. It is therefore the combination of the different thicknesses of thread plus the type of stitch used that gives variety to the tone and texture of the embroidery. Smooth, plain-coloured or variegated threads are preferable to the highly twisted or textured varieties; these can prove difficult to handle and detract from the lacy effects of the stitches.

Use special ballpoint needles for working the needlepoint. These will slip easily under the threads without piercing either the stitch or the ground fabric. Work the prepared design either pinned to a bobbin lace pillow or in the hand.

You will need

For a picture, 22cm by 26cm, including the frame

30cm of 90cm-wide unbleached calico
34cm by 34cm of natural-coloured hessian
34cm by 34cm of heavy-weight interlining
Matching sewing threads
One skein each of Anchor stranded cotton in the following colours: 0131, 0161, 0128, 0402, 086, 0360, 0352, 0392, 0390, 0398, 0255, 0239, 0268, 0214, 0288, 0291
20cm by 24cm of polyvinyl chloride (an adhesive acetate film from drawing-office suppliers)
22cm by 26cm of 3mm-thick card

1 Treble Brussels-corded
2 Inverted pyramids
3 Alençon mesh-whipped stitch
4 Ardenza point
5 Corded filling
6 Treble Brussels
7 Pea stitch
8 Pea stitch variation
9 Spanish ground
10 Point de Grecque bar

1sq = 1cm

No. 5 crewel needle
Milward's ballpoint needles
Lace pillow
All-purpose clear adhesive
Cartridge paper

Preparing to work

Scale up the design given below and follow Working the needlepoint to step 1. Then, following the colour guide and step 2, begin to lay the cordonnet in the appropriate colours. Use double six-stranded thread for the cord and couch with a single strand in the same colour.

Using a ballpoint needle and following the stitch key, begin to work the filling stitches. Embroider the different shades of colour working from side to side, remembering that the length of thread in your needle should be long enough to reach across the stitch area. It is therefore not possible to join a new thread in the middle of a row. A variety of different tones can be achieved by working lacy types of stitches contrasted with very solid stitches. Or, alternatively, by using the same coloured thread and working the same stitch either close together or far apart.

With three strands of thread doubled and buttonholing with two strands, work the second cord, called the cordonnette, and complete step 3 of Working the needlepoint.

Making the frame

Transfer the outline of the arch on to card, draw a second line 3cm outside it and cut out the frame. Remove the window area carefully. Place the frame centrally on the interlining and cut it out leaving 1.5cm turnings all round. Fold the turnings to the wrong side, snipping into corners and curves and then glue in place. Repeat in exactly the same way for the hessian.

For the window sill, cut a rectangle of card 6cm by 15cm. Score three lines across, each 1.5cm apart, and fold to form the window sill. Cover with interlining and hessian, allowing extra hessian at each side to cover the short ends and glue in place. Leave to dry before attaching the window sill with clear adhesive.

Embroider the wall plants around the frame using straight stitch, chain stitch and French knots. Work the stems first and the leaves on top.

Making up

Pin the picture to the back of the frame. Bring the window sill lace over the shaped sill and hem the picture in place stitching the outer cord to the hessian frame. Back the picture with calico, neatly slip stitching around the edge. Attach a brass ring for hanging.

Working the needlepoint

1 Transfer the motif on to writing paper and outline with black felt-tipped pen. Cut a piece of acetate film to the same size as the paper, remove the backing and place it centrally over the traced motif. Cut a piece of calico twice the size of the design, plus 5cm all round, for the backing. Turn in and tack the raw edges. Fold the calico in half and tack together. Place the prepared motif centrally on the calico backing and tack through to hold.

2 The cordonnet is laid in a continuous line so that the finished motif will hold together in one piece. Cut a thread twice the measurement around the motif and fold in half. Begin with the looped end and using sewing cotton and a crewel needle, couch it through all the layers with stitches 2mm apart. Where two lines meet, take one strand of the cordonnet through the laid cord and continue. To finish, thread the cord through the starting loop, cut, fold the end back and couch them together.

3 Pin the motif to a cushion and, using fine thread and a ballpoint needle, complete the filling stitches. To give a well-raised outline, buttonhole a second double thread (the cordonette) over the first cordonnet. Using the same technique as before, buttonhole with a fine thread and with the looped edge facing outwards. Remove the motif from the support, snip the tacks and couching stitches between the two layers of calico and ease the lace away. Remove any short threads with a pair of tweezers.

Needlepoint fillings

The stitches used to fill the areas between the lines formed by the cordonnet are mainly variations of buttonhole filling — that is, buttonhole stitch worked without entering the background fabric. (For the purpose of simplicity, the cordonnet is shown as a single line and without couching.) Work all filling stitches with a finer thread than the cordonnet.

Beginning and finishing the buttonhole thread

All needlepoint filling stitches should be started and finished in this way. At a short distance below the starting point, slip the needle between the two strands of the cordonnet, under the couching stitches, and bring it out at the correct position. Take it round one strand to secure it lightly; it will be held quite firmly when the cordonnet is worked later. Make sure your thread is sufficiently long to work a complete row.

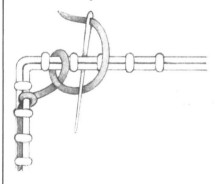

Working from left to right, complete the first row. At the side edge, take the thread under and over the cordonnet ready to begin the next row, returning from right to left. In some cases, e.g. in Treble Brussels, you will need to take the thread round the cordonnet more than once to reach the correct depth. Complete the filling and finish in the same way.

Treble Brussels

1 Work groups of three buttonhole stitches over the cordonnet, leaving between each group a loop of the same width as that of the three stitches together.

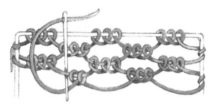

2 On the next and subsequent rows, work similar groups of three stitches over the loops formed in the previous row.

Corded treble Brussels

This stitch is a variation of both Treble Brussels and Corded filling.

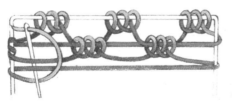

Work the first row as for Treble Brussels, over the cordonnet. On the return row take the thread back to the opposite edge and round the cordonnet. Now work groups of three stitches, taking the needle behind the loop formed in the first row and the straight thread at the same time and repeat to fill the required space.

Inverted pyramids

This stitch is worked from the base of the pyramid downwards, but by turning the embroidery and working from the bottom of the space upwards, you could make upright pyramids instead.

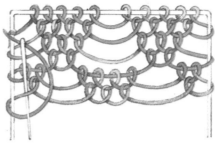

Begin with a row of close buttonhole stitches — the number of stitches required for the base of each pyramid plus one spacing stitch for each pyramid. On the return row work four stitches into the five loops formed in the previous row. Miss the next loop, work the same number of stitches into the following loops and repeat to the end of the row.

Work back across the loops as before, working one less stitch into each group and thus making a longer loop across the space between each pyramid.

Repeat on the next two, working two stitches in each pyramid to form the peak.

On the next row, work the required number of stitches for the base of the pyramid over the long loop between the pairs of stitches worked in the previous row. Work compensating stitches at the side edges as shown and complete the filling. Take care to make the stitches of equal length and do not allow the pyramids to become slack. This is important in the case of the last loop, which holds the next group of stitches.

Alençon mesh (whipped stitch)

Work a row of evenly spaced buttonhole stitches over the cordonnet and secure it to the right.

1 Take the thread under the last loop of the first row, whipping over and under every loop to the end of the row. Adjust each stitch as it is worked; do not try to pull the thread straight at the end, as this will cause the buttonhole stitches to become twisted as they are worked.

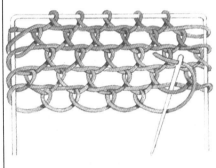

2 On the return journey work a buttonhole stitch over each loop made in the first row — but not over the whipping thread. Repeat rows 1 and 2 to fill the space.

Ardenza point

This stitch is made up from a series of double buttonhole stitches worked as a mesh filling.

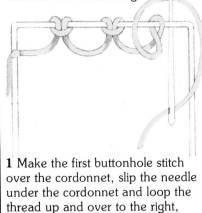

1 Make the first buttonhole stitch over the cordonnet, slip the needle under the cordonnet and loop the thread up and over to the right,

under the point of the needle. Pull the needle gently downwards to secure the stitches, then take it to the right, about the same distance as the width of the double buttonhole stitch ready to make a second pair of stitches. Repeat the action to the end of the row.

2 Make a double buttonhole stitch over the loop between the last two stitches of the previous row and continue to the end. Repeat row 2 to fill the space.

Ardenza point bar

1 Attach thread at left. Take across to the opposite side, stitch once around the cordonnet and bring it back to the starting point. Work the first row as for Ardenza point.

2 Turn the work around and work a second row of Ardenza point over the cordonnet and between the stitches made in the first row.

Pea stitch

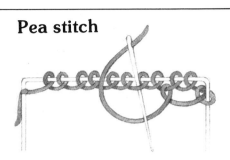

1 Begin with a row of buttonhole stitches worked in pairs over the cordonnet, making the spaces between equal to the width of the two stitches. Work a single buttonhole stitch into the loop before the last pair of stitches in the previous row. Continue to work single stitches into the loops between each pair of stitches to the end of the row.

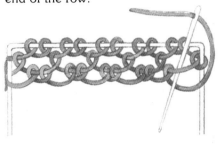

2 Work a pair of buttonhole stitches into the loops between the stitches of the previous row and repeat rows 2 and 3 to fill the space.

Pea stitch variation

1 Begin by working evenly spaced buttonhole stitches over the top cordonnet. On the return journey, work two buttonhole stitches into the loops made in the previous row. Miss two loops and then continue to work pairs of stitches alternately to the end of the row.

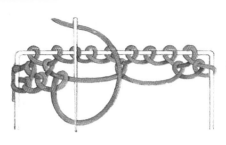

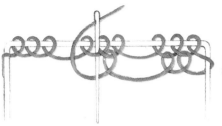

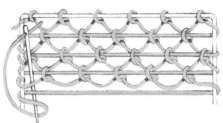

2 Work the first stitch into the loop after the last stitch in the previous row, then work the next stitch through the short loop. Now work three stitches over the long loop lying between the first and second pairs of stitches and repeat to the end of the row.

2 On the next row, work two buttonhole stitches into the loops between each group of three stitches made in the previous row and repeat to the end of the row.

2 Make the second and subsequent rows of knots by working into the loops of the first row and the straight thread. Continue to the end and repeat steps 2 and 3 to fill the required space.

Corded filling

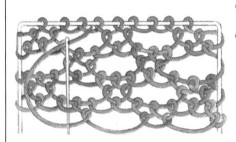

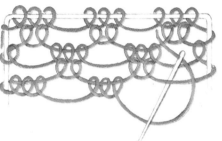

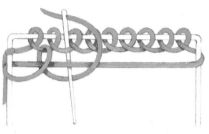

3 Work two stitches into the loops between the three stitches made in the previous row and continue to the end. Repeat rows 2 and 3 to fill the space.

3 Working into the half loop of the previous row, make a single stitch and then continue to work three stitches over the loop between the pairs of stitches. Repeat to the end of the row, working a single stitch over the last loop before the cordonnet. Repeat rows 2 and 3 to fill the space.

1 Work buttonhole stitches closely and evenly along the cordonnet. Take the thread back to just below the starting point and round the cordonnet at the opposite side.

Spanish ground

Point de Grecque bar

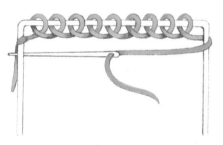

1 Begin by working groups of three buttonhole stitches over the cordonnet, leaving a space between each group the same width as the three stitches together.

1 Begin with a single buttonhole stitch at the top left corner. Take the thread a short distance along the cordonnet, and after making a small loop, take the needle behind the cordonnet and back through the loop as shown. Pull the thread gently to form a knot. Continue making evenly spaced knots to the end. Bring the thread back and wrap it twice around the cordonnet.

2 Work the second and following rows of buttonhole stitches, taking the needle behind a loop and the straight thread at the same time and continue to fill the space.

Tape lace camisole

**This beautifully stitched camisole, in polyester crêpe, has fine
rouleau straps and a pretty inset edging of flowers made from lacy
tape and needlepoint stitches.**

Materials

Tape lace, as its name implies, requires
a foundation of ready-made tape
which can be bought from specialist
suppliers. These tapes are usually
white or cream and are woven in a
variety of patterns and in different
widths from 3mm to 8mm wide. They
can be plain, picot edged or have a
pattern of mock faggoting woven
down the middle. Plain haberdasher's
lace can be used quite successfully
although it is heavier and requires a
certain amount of care in handling,
particularly in shaping tight curves.

Take care to use stainless steel pins
on fine fabrics to prevent rust marks,
and large holes from appearing. Use

a reasonably fine thread for the embroidered filling stitches such as sewing thread, single strands of embroidery cotton or silk, coton à broder or fine pearl threads.

You will need

For a camisole, to fit 91cm bust

4m of 1cm-wide cream tape
70cm of 90cm-wide cream polyester crêpe
One reel of matching sewing thread
Tacking thread in a contrast colour
Crewel needle
Ballpoint needle
Stiff brown paper
6mm-wide white elastic to fit waist
1m of white 1.5cm-wide bias binding
Dressmaker's graph paper
(See page 156 for the address of a specialist tape supplier)

To make

Trace off the design given opposite reversing it on the centre line as indicated. Strengthen the outline with a black waterproof marker.

Cut the brown paper to size and following the instructions in Working tape lace, complete steps 1, 2 and 3.

Work the couronnes (separate buttonholed rings) as for the first stage of spider rings attaching the rings only, to complete the lace edge.

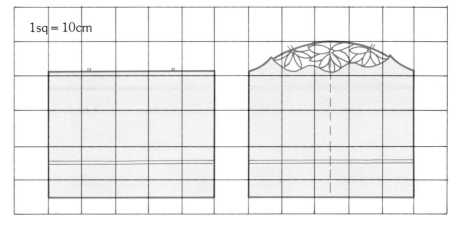

1sq = 10cm

Using dressmaker's graph paper, transfer the camisole front section and cut it out. (One square equals 10cm.)

Cut the crêpe fabric in half to give two pieces measuring 45cm by 50cm. Place the paper pattern on the fabric and cut it out. Pin the finished lace edge centrally to the top edge of the front section and tack in place. Machine close zigzag stitch around the edge with matching thread. Using very sharp-pointed scissors, and taking care not to cut the embroidery, trim away the fabric from behind the lace.

Begin by cutting away the bulk of the fabric leaving a small margin at the lower edge. Then, rolling the excess fabric away from the edge, trim close to the zigzag stitching.

Attach the back section to the front joining both side edges with flat fell seams. Trim the top edge of the back section level with the underarm curve. Make a 5mm double turning and hand stitch around, gently curving the front arm section into the seam.

Make two bias-cut rouleau straps, each 43cm long. Neatly hand stitch them in place at the points indicated. Try on and mark the waist level with pins. Working on the wrong side, apply bias binding to fit and then remove the pins. Machine stitch both sides, leaving a small opening at the seam to insert the elastic. Make a 6mm double turning on the hem and hand stitch. Insert the elastic and overcast the edges to finish.

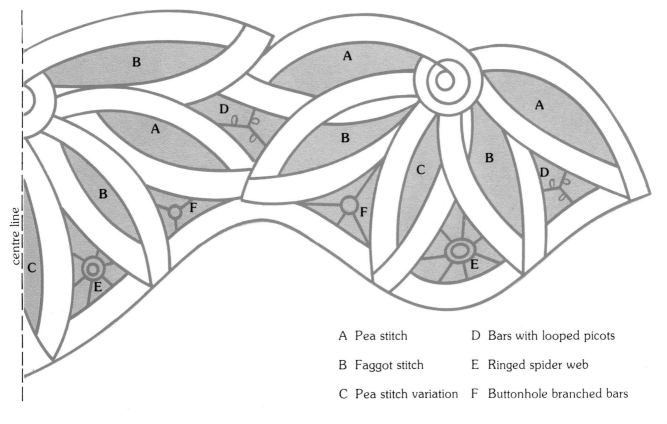

A Pea stitch

B Faggot stitch

C Pea stitch variation

D Bars with looped picots

E Ringed spider web

F Buttonhole branched bars

Working tape lace

 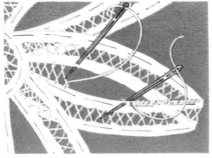 

1 Cut a piece of thick brown paper twice the size of the design, fold it in half and tack together. Transfer the design to the brown paper. Lay the tape right-side down in as continuous a line as possible, and tack down the centre using small stitches. Adjust the tape around all the curves keeping the outside edges flat.

2 With wrong side uppermost, and using a crewel needle with matching thread, whip stitch around the edges. Stitch about 2.5cm at a time pulling up the curved edges to reduce fullness. Continue to whip all round the design stitching crossings and joins together. Using a ballpoint needle, work the filling stitches. Begin the first stitch with a very small knot and overcast once. Continue to work Faggot stitch, for example, as shown in the centre of the petal.

3 Complete all the fillings, spider webs and bars, as given in the diagram, remembering that the lace is facing right-side down. For Pea stitch and Pea stitch variation, see page 18. Turn the paper over and remove all the tacking threads. Make separate buttonholed rings (couronnes) and attach them to the right side. Work French knots in the middle to finish, if preferred.

Ring spider web

The ring spider web is the simplest of spider webs. It can be used to strengthen large cut areas and yet produce a very delicate, lacy effect.

1 First make a small detached ring by winding the thread two or three times around a knitting needle. Slip it off the needle and finish with buttonholing.

2 Pin the ring in place and attach it to the surrounding fabric with twisted bars. Take a single thread from the ring to the fabric, secure with a small stitch, and twist it back to the centre ring.

3 Run the thread through the buttonhole loops on the outside of the ring and on to the next position. Continue to work four or five bars to complete the web.

Buttonholed branched bars

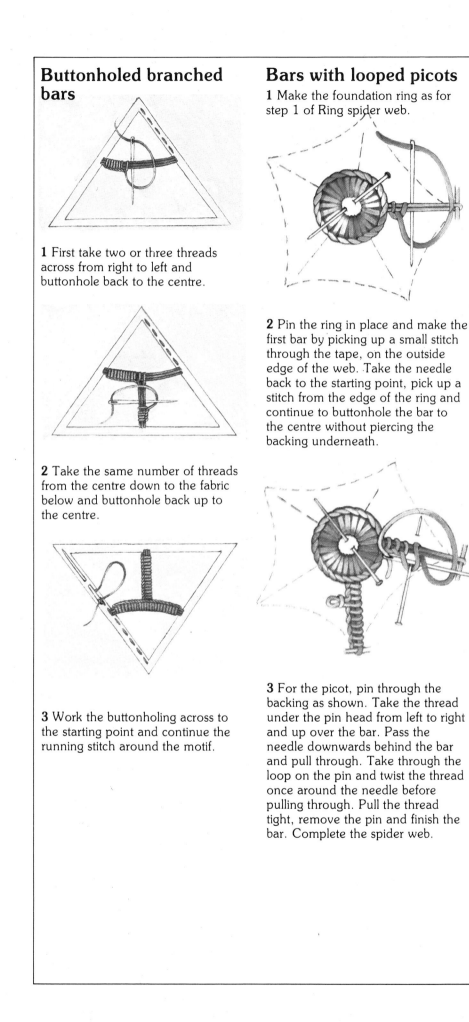

1 First take two or three threads across from right to left and buttonhole back to the centre.

2 Take the same number of threads from the centre down to the fabric below and buttonhole back up to the centre.

3 Work the buttonholing across to the starting point and continue the running stitch around the motif.

Bars with looped picots

1 Make the foundation ring as for step 1 of Ring spider web.

2 Pin the ring in place and make the first bar by picking up a small stitch through the tape, on the outside edge of the web. Take the needle back to the starting point, pick up a stitch from the edge of the ring and continue to buttonhole the bar to the centre without piercing the backing underneath.

3 For the picot, pin through the backing as shown. Take the thread under the pin head from left to right and up over the bar. Pass the needle downwards behind the bar and pull through. Take through the loop on the pin and twist the thread once around the needle before pulling through. Pull the thread tight, remove the pin and finish the bar. Complete the spider web.

Faggot-stitch

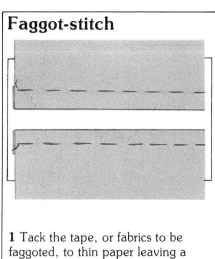

1 Tack the tape, or fabrics to be faggoted, to thin paper leaving a gap of 5mm for the faggoting stitch. The distance between the two edges will need to be greater for a more elaborate stitch, or for stitches worked in a thicker thread.

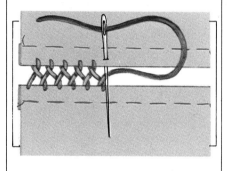

2 Fasten the thread with tiny back stitches on the wrong side of the fabric at the end of the open seam. Begin the stitch by bringing the needle out near the end of the seam on the right side of the fabric. Take diagonally across to the opposite edge and insert into the right side of the fabric as shown.

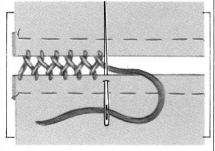

3 Pull the thread through, holding it in place with the left thumb. Take the needle over the working thread and insert into the right side of the fabric on the opposite edge. Pass the needle over working thread as before and repeat. Work with an even tension throughout.

Tenerife lace collar

Transform a plain neck edge with this exquisite lace collar made
in subtle shades of natural coloured cotton. Thread it with cream
satin ribbon.

Materials

The same fine cotton and linen threads produced for crochet and bobbin lace are ideal for making Tenerife lace.

These threads are graded according to their thickness and are available in a range of sizes, and in a variety of natural colours from white, cream, écru and buff. The range of brighter colours in these fine threads is somewhat limited, but small amounts of embroidery thread may be used quite successfully at the second stage of Tenerife lacemaking when the basic threads are stitched together in a decorative pattern.

For this embroidery use either single strands of coton à broder, silk, rayon or multiple strands of stranded embroidery cotton, in plain or variegated colours. Experiment with fine crewel or two-ply knitting yarn and gold and silver threads.

In order to slide the embroidery needle under the threads easily, a round-pointed tapestry needle is recommended; choose a small size for very fine threads.

You will need

For a collar, 36cm (neck edge) by 7.5cm deep

One ball of natural écru DMC Cordonnet Spécial, No. 60
One skein of cream Anchor stranded cotton 0388
1m of 3mm-wide cream satin ribbon
No. 16 tapestry needle
Brass or stainless steel pins
Clear adhesive
Four or five polystyrene ceiling tiles
Heavy tracing paper
Wallpaper paste

Making the block

First stick the polystyrene tiles together with wallpaper paste to make a suitable working block. It should be deep enough to take the full length of the pins, plus a little clearance.

Trace off the circular lace motif given below, and pin to the block.

Circular motif

With the required length of thread in the needle, and following Knotting Tenerife lace, work the motif to the first row of knotting. Following the stitch detail given, take the working thread outwards to the third circle on the diagram and work a similar row of knotting over the same pairs of threads as in the previous row. Finish row as before and move on to the outer circle, next to the pins. Work another row of knot stitch joining together the two threads between each pin, thus forming a neat zigzag pattern. Repeat working a second row close to the last, finishing with an extra knot. Cut off the thread close to the work and secure with the smallest spot of glue applied with the point of a pin.

Using three strands of the Anchor embroidery cotton in the needle, and approximately 140cm long, work the flower in knot stitch beginning with the petal nearest point B. Secure the thread at the base of the petal to the left thread at point B. Following the petal shape, work knot stitch over each single thread and finish as before. Work a second row outside the first neatening the cut ends of thread with tiny spots of glue, as before.

Remove all the pins and neaten the threads on the back of the motif.

It should be possible to re-use the paper pattern several times. Move its position with each motif to prevent the pins from pitting and weakening the surface of the polystyrene.

Make eight more similar motifs.

Neck band

Trace off the neck band pattern given on page 26 and fasten it to the board. Place pins through the points marked around both edges of the neck band. The basic threads are attached and taken around the pins in a very similar way to the circular motif but without crossing in the centre. Using the DMC cotton throughout complete the foundation threads, starting at A, as shown on the opposite page.

Beginning at the left, with the inner neck edge facing, work the first row of knot stitch joining together the two threads between each pin.

Following the stitch detail given for the neck band, work the overcast bars next over four threads. Begin with a

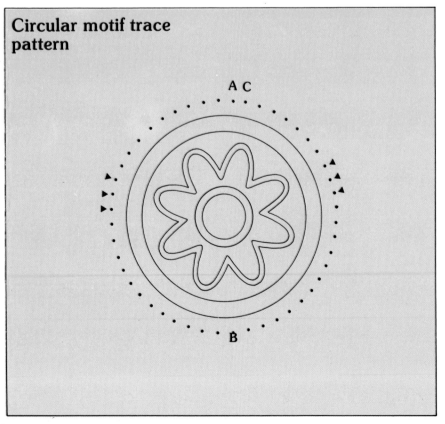

Circular motif trace pattern

A C

B

Tenerife lace

knot, overcast to the required depth and finish with a second knot. Take the thread on to the next group of threads and overcast downwards finishing with a knot. Take the thread to the top of the bar, make a second knot and repeat until the second bar under the woven triangle is reached. Take the thread to the top of the triangle and knot four threads together (the inner two threads from each bar below the triangle). Now, needleweave downwards finishing with a knot. Repeat to complete the ribbon slots. Work the final row of knot stitch joining together pairs of threads between pins, to give a scalloped edge. Use the woven triangles in which to hide a joined thread, otherwise knot neatly and neaten the ends with glue.

Finally, place the circular motifs and the neck band in position and oversew the loops together as indicated in the diagram. Neaten the ends. Thread ribbon through the slots to finish.

Stitch details

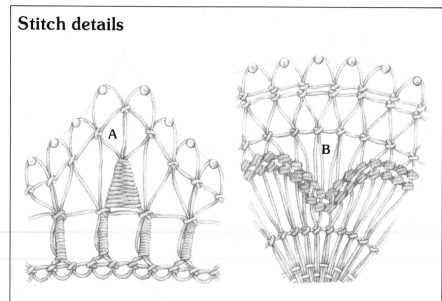

A Neck band stitch detail shows overcast bars between rows of knot stitch and woven bars.

B Circular motif stitch detail shows rows of knot stitches forming lacy construction and petal shapes.

Neck band trace pattern

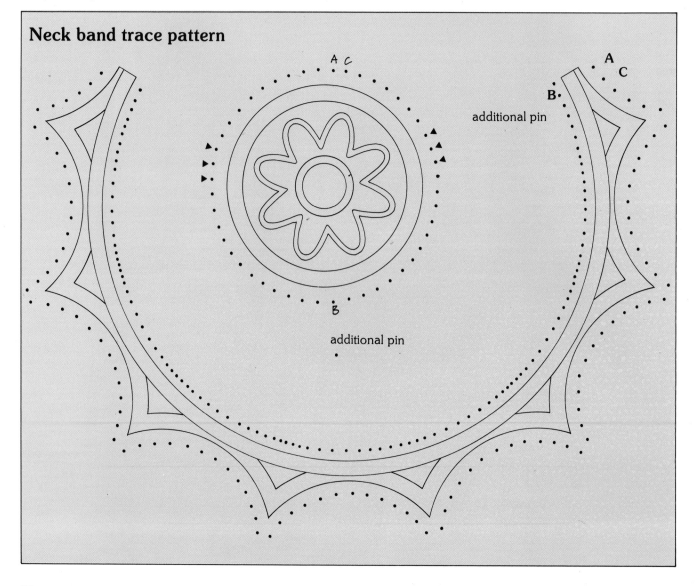

additional pin

additional pin

Knotting Tenerife lace

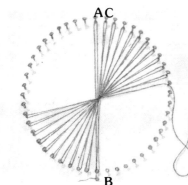

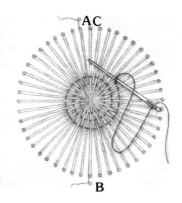

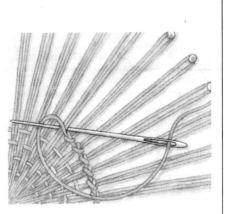

1 With the design secured to a block of polystyrene, mark each point around the outer edge with pins and push them half-way down. Add an extra pin below point B. Working from the ball of thread, secure one end to the pin and push it down out of the way. Continue to wind thread around the pin at A working from left to right, then down to B from right to left, and up to C, and so on, to fill the circle, crossing the threads only in the middle. Take the thread across the circle, cut it and secure temporarily outside the circle. Push the pins well down.

2 For darning the centre, use approximately 230cm of thread in the needle. Begin in the middle by leaving a long end which will be trimmed later on. Hold the centre of the threads with a finger, and working from right to left, weave under and over pairs of threads starting at B. Complete the first row and pull tight, manipulating it with the point of the needle to centralize, if necessary. Weave five rows to complete the inner circle. To secure the weaving take the needle under the previous row at point B, and then take it along the pair of threads to where they intersect the next circle ready to begin knotting. Do not pull the thread too tightly.

3 This row of knot stitch is worked over pairs of threads beginning at B. Working from right to left, pass the needle behind the first pair of threads, and with the working thread looped around the needle point, bring through and pull tight. Make sure that the knot is in the right position with the correct distance between the pairs of threads before tightening. Complete the circle and secure the last stitch by working over the first knot. Continue with the same working thread, taking it to next intersection as previously described.

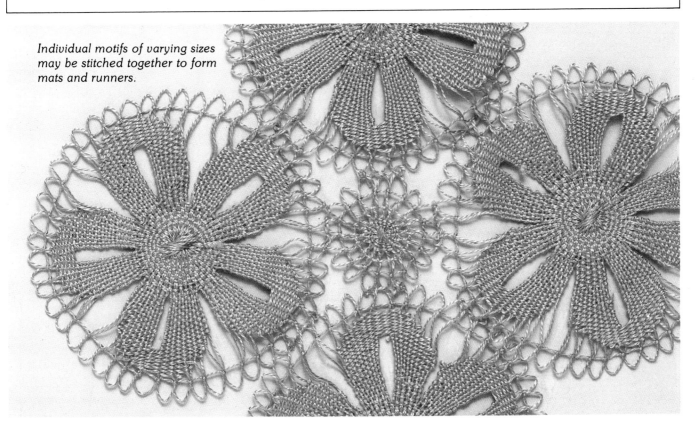

Individual motifs of varying sizes may be stitched together to form mats and runners.

Chapter 2

Bobbin Lace

Traditionally surrounded by mystery and romance, bobbin lace is arguably one of the prettiest and most versatile of laces. It can produce both edgings and fabric in the delicacy of Bedfordshire lace and the chunkier textures of Torchon.

It involves working on a pillow, plaiting and twisting separate threads in pattern, using as few as nine bobbins, but often many more. Once the 'knack' of handling the bobbins has been mastered, even a beginner will soon develop speed and a smooth rhythm of working. Here it is important to keep the bobbins that are not in use pinned well away from the working area.

The information given in the following pages is structured as a series of lessons, progressing from simple Torchon edgings to leaves and tallies used in Bedfordshire lace. Each lesson finishes with a project incorporating those particular skills. There are lots of patterns for pretty edgings, lavender bags, bookmarks and mats, to delight beginners and enthusiasts alike.

Simple Torchon

Bobbin lacemaking may at first sight appear to be very complicated and difficult. But appearances are deceptive. Even the complete beginner can soon learn to make pretty and delicate lace edgings.

In addition to the traditional English styles of bobbin lace — the most famous being Honiton, Bedfordshire and Buckinghamshire — other laces common to most European countries were Torchon lace (Torchon being the French for 'dishcloth'), which is geometric in character, and Tape lace, where a few pairs of bobbins were worked together to form a braid or 'tape' that was later hand-stitched into a flowing pattern (see page 20). All these styles and types of lace are still made today.

Equipment

Pillow This can vary in size, but the easiest to learn on is rectangular in shape. It consists of a bag, made in calico or a similar tough fabric, into which a board to the same size is slipped to provide a firm base for the work. A large amount of wood wool or straw is stuffed into the bag, on top of the board, packed so tight that a thumb print leaves no impression.

A dark coloured cover for the pillow will ensure that it keeps clean and shows up the lace threads to best advantage.

Pillows are available ready-made, or it is a fairly simple matter to make one yourself.

Bobbins Bobbins are usually made in wood. Plastic bobbins are available but because they are light in weight, are far less satisfying to work with.

The shapes easiest for beginners to manipulate are called Midlands' bobbins. These are basically pieces of wood with a narrower turned area at one end of the shank for the thread, and a loop of wire hung with beads threaded through a hole at the other to give the bobbin weight. Young mothers used to put the buttons from their first baby's boots on their bobbins.

The beads — or whatever is used — are called the 'spangle'. Unless you are an expert wood turner, it is best to buy the bobbins from one of the many bobbin makers and lace specialists, most of whom offer a mail order service (see page 156).

Pins Lacemaking pins are always longer in length, made in brass and sold in two thicknesses. The thicker variety can be used for simple basic patterns, but once you progress to more delicate work, it is advisable to use the finer brass pins. Do not use those made of steel; they may rust, so ruining hours of labour.

Thread Traditionally all lace was made in linen thread. Nowadays this is less easy to find, especially in the finer

weights. Cotton threads are generally available in a good range however. Synthetic threads are not good to use as they tend to stretch. The correct thread is always given at the begining of any pattern. Use an alternative and the lace would end up looking either too sparse or too lumpy.

Pattern This is called a 'pricking'. In order to make a pricking, you will need the special waxed pricking card and a pricker, which is basically a needle set into a wooden handle.

Cover cloths These should be in dark smooth cotton and are used to protect the work, or to help in moving the lace up the pillow in order to start a new section.

Learning the stitches

Before embarking on the Little Torchon fan trimming, a beginner should practise making the stitches, and for this you will need:
12 bobbins
Lace pillow
Pricking card and pricker
Graph paper with 10 squares per 2.5cm
Pencil
Brass pins
Thread — DMC Fil à Dentelles (cotton)
Cover cloths

Winding a bobbin
To wind a bobbin, hold it with the left hand with the narrow part or 'long neck' towards the right. With the right hand, wind the thread on to the bobbin evenly and tightly, winding over and away from you.

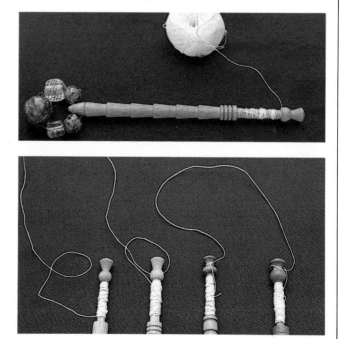

Making a hitch
Having wound about 1m of thread on to the bobbin, pull out the same length from the ball and cut off. Working from the cut end, wind the thread on to a second bobbin, again winding over and away from you in a clockwise direction. When there is about 15cm of thread between the bobbins, make a hitch on the thread of each bobbin to secure it. This prevents the thread from unwinding off the bobbin, while allowing for more thread to be unwound as required. Wind six pairs of bobbins in all.

Making the pattern

To make a pattern for the basic stitches, cut a piece of graph paper 23cm by 2.5cm. Mark the position of the pin holes as shown. Cut a piece of pricking card to the same size and pin it to the pillow with the graph paper on top. Prick holes through the marks and remove the graph paper. Pin the pricking down the centre of the pillow, starting about 5-7.5cm from the top of the pillow. Cover the cloth and pin it tightly to the pillow on either side.

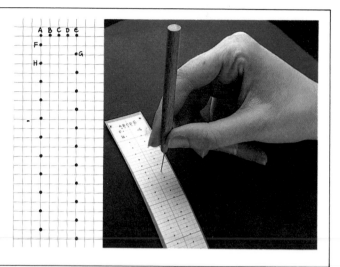

Cloth stitch (cs)

1 Place pins in the holes numbered A-F and hang a pair of bobbins from each one. Using the pairs from F and A, make a cloth stitch (cs). Number the position of the bobbins from 1 to 4 in your own mind. The numbers refer to the positions, not to the bobbins. Start by lifting the bobbin in position 2 over that in position 3. Next, using both hands together, lift 2 over 1 and 4 over 3. Finish by lifting 2 over 3. One cloth stitch has now been completed and the first two pairs of bobbins have changed place.

2 To repeat the stitch, push the left hand pair out of the way to the left of the work and take the pairs from F and B. Repeat the movements to make another cloth stitch, then move the left-hand pair to the left as before. Continue right across using the threads from C, D and E. The threads hanging from F (the 'weavers') have now travelled across the pattern, passing through all the other pairs (the 'passives'). Twist the weavers by lifting the right-hand thread of the weaving pair over the left-hand thread, then repeat the move.

3 To work back across the row, insert a pin in the hole marked G to the left of the weavers. Now work back along the row. Make a cloth stitch using the same movements with the weavers and the pair from E. Once completed, push the right-hand pair to the right before taking the next pair from D. Once the weavers reach the left of the pattern, twist the weavers twice, right over left, then place a pin in hole H to the right of the weavers.

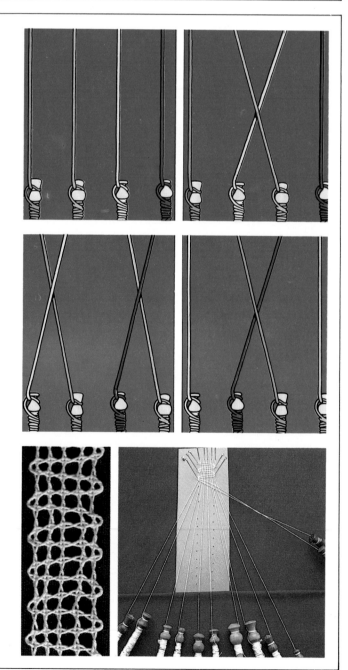

Cloth stitch and twist (cst)

Whichever way you are weaving, whether from left to right or right to left, the cloth stitch and the twists are always worked the same way, only the sides from which you take the fresh pair alter. This applies equally to the cloth stitch and twist (cst), which is a variation of cloth stitch. Work one stitch in the normal way, then twist each pair once, right over the left, that is repeating the second movement. At the end of a row there will be one twist on the weavers already; put on one more for a total of two.

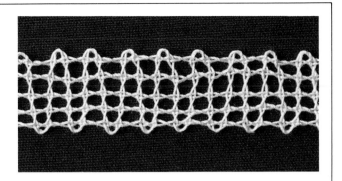
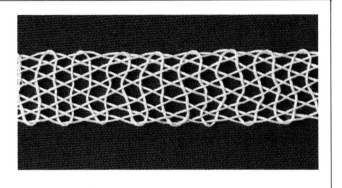

Half stitch (hs)

The second basic stitch is known as half stitch (hs). Work the first two movements of a cloth stitch only, travelling across the row as before. All the threads will lie twisted right over left as in cloth stitch and twist. Before inserting the pin, twist the weavers once more making two twists in all. Only one of the weavers will have travelled across the row; all the other threads are travelling diagonally. To ensure an even tension and straight edges, hold the weavers firmly at the end of each row after inserting a pin; stroke the passives down. Practise stitches until they become automatic.

Moving up the lace

When you reach the bottom of the pricking, move the cover cloth down as necessary, pin the threads to it carefully. Fold the cover cloth over the bobbins to take the tension off the threads, then take the pins out of the pricking. Lift the lace to the top of the pricking, then replace the first 4-5cm of the pins. Unpin the bobbins and continue working; try not to pull the passives to begin with.

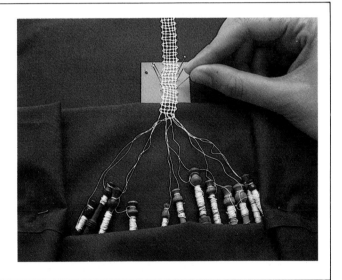

Abbreviations

The following abbreviations are used in bobbin lace patterns:

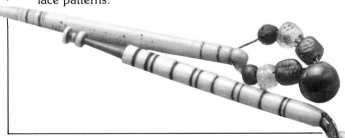

A, B, C	the letters of the alphabet are used to identify the pinholes from which the bobbins are hung
1, 2, 3 a, b, c	either numerals or lower case letters, or both, are used to identify the pinholes of one pattern repeat
cs	cloth stitch
cst	cloth stitch twist
hs	half stitch
tw	twist

Trimming in Little Torchon fan

The patterns in the first three projects are for Torchon lace. Use the basic stitches you have just learned to make the first, called Little Torchon fan.

Abbreviations
See page 33

You will need
For a narrow trim, 2cm wide

Basic equipment (as previously given)
Bocken's linen thread No. 5
Fine waterproof felt-tipped pen or ink pen

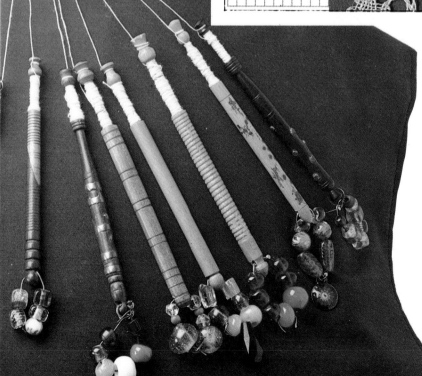

Preparing to work
Wind eight pairs of bobbins as described on page 30 and make a pricking paper for the pattern shown below. Mark the pinhole numbers of the first repeat pattern on the card for easy reference. Use a felt-tipped or ink pen as a ballpoint or pencil might mark the lace with constant nibbing.

Hang three pairs of bobbins on the pin marked as A, one each on B and C, two on D and one on E.

Making the lace
Pinholes 1, 4 and 6 create the straight edging called the 'foot'; 2, 3 and 5 make up the 'net', and 7-16 form the 'fan' pattern.

Pinhole 1 This is a 'foot' pin. With the 3rd pair from the right (from A), work through the 2 pairs to the right of it in cst. Put the pin in the hole

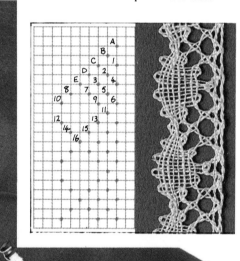

between the 2nd and 3rd pairs from the right and work another cst with these 2 pairs.

Pinhole 2 With the left-hand pair from 1, and the pair from B, work hs, insert pin, work another hs with the same 2 pairs.

Pinhole 3 With the left-hand pair from 2, and the pair from C, work hs, insert pin, work another hs with the same 2 pairs.

Take out pins A, B, and C; carefully pull down the loops that are left.

Pinhole 4 As pinhole 1.

Pinhole 5 As pinhole 2, using left-hand and pair from 4 and right-hand pair from 3.

Pinhole 6 As pinhole 1.

Pinhole 7 Work the pair from E (weavers) to the right in cs through 3 pairs. Twist weavers twice and insert pin in between weavers and last pair passed through.

Pinhole 8 Work back to the left, through the same three pairs in cs, then twist weavers twice and insert pin between the weavers and the last pair passed through.

Pinhole 9 As pinhole 7, but work through 4 pairs.

Pinhole 10 As pinhole 8, but work through 4 pairs.

Pinhole 11 As pinhole 7, but work through 5 pairs.

Pinhole 12 As pinhole 8, but work through 5 pairs.

Pinhole 13 As pinhole 7, but work through 4 pairs.

Pinhole 14 As pinhole 8, but work through 4 pairs.

Pinhole 15 As pinhole 7, but work through 3 pairs.

Pinhole 16 As pinhole 8, but work through 3 pairs.

Take out pin D and pull down the loops. Twist each of the pairs hanging at 11, 13 and 15 once, right over left. You have now completed one pattern repeat. Continue working the pattern repeat until you have the correct length of lace required.

Finishing off
Finishing at the end of a pattern repeat, carefully reef knot each bobbin with its partner so that the knots lie really close to the last line of pins in the pattern.

Cut the bobbins off the pillow, leaving ends of threads about 7.5cm long after the reef knots.

When applying the trimming to a fabric, insert these ends into the seam or catch them down on to the underside of the fabric.

Fir tree fan and spider

The Fir tree fan edging and the bookmark are both made from Torchon lace, a versatile form of bobbin lace found in most European countries. Torchon lace can be made with either coarse or fine thread and is equally well suited for trimming baby clothes or edging table linen.

Fir tree fan

This is a traditional pattern and contains a typical fan shape (see also page 34 for the Little Torchon fan). There are a number of different ways of working the fan, which may vary in size depending on the width of the lace and the number of pairs of bobbins involved. Once the basic fan has been mastered, it is possible to experiment, using different stitches.

The pattern is normally called Fir tree because the markings on the pricking look rather like a child's drawing of a fir tree. In its basic form, as shown here, it is the same pattern as that used for the lace which trimmed Oliver Cromwell's baby clothes.

Insertion lace

In the old days lace was often worked with a foot on both sides, instead of having the footside on the right and the headside on the left. This enabled it to be sewn on both sides so that it could be inserted into lingerie or table linen or used to trim garments.

It is quite easy to turn this type of lace into a bookmark, with both sides extended diagonally at each end to make a point and with an imitation foot edge worked on the diagonals.

Spiders

Spiders or snowflakes, as they are sometimes called, were used in the bookmark. A popular component of many Torchon patterns, spiders give an open appearance to lace and can be worked quite quickly.

Working the Fir tree fan

This may vary in size, but six pairs are used here — two from a (weavers and outermost passives) and four pairs from existing work. Work weavers from a to b through four pairs in cst (see page 33). Twist weavers once more and insert pin in b. Return to pin c through four pairs.

Continue working through one pair less on each pair of rows until g is reached. From g to h the weavers work through all passives, plus one more pair in cst, but with an extra twist on the weavers only after each stitch. Repeat for h to j. The second half of the fan is a mirror image of the first.

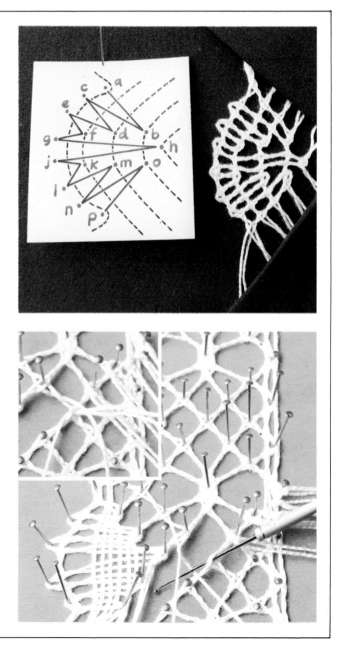

Joining lace

When the lace is almost complete, pin the first 2cm-3cm of pattern carefully back into position, pushing all the pins right in. Complete the lace. At the point where the pairs should go to work the next stitch, take the pin out of the hole and push a crochet hook through the little loop. Draw back one of the threads of the pair and put the partner bobbin through the loop thus made. Tighten the threads, put the pin back and tie a reef knot.

Imitation foot edge

Place two support pins in the pillow above A.
Hang a pair of bobbins from each. With them
work hs (see page 33), insert pin in A, hs.
Remove support pins. Hang a pair on a support
pin above 1 and repeat, using a new pair and the
left-hand pair from A. Repeat for 2 and all down
the left-hand side, each time using a new pair and
the left-hand pair from the previous pin. Go back
to A and repeat for a, using a new pair and the
right-hand pair from A. Continue down the right-
hand side.

Setting in passives

Make an extra pinhole (x) midway between
pinholes 1 and a. Hang two pairs of bobbins on
this pin, in the centre of the other pairs, so that
the second pair lies outside the first. Twist the left-
hand pair once and work it in cst through the
pairs hanging from 1, 2, 3 and so on until it lies
one pair in from the edge. Repeat, working to the
right with the right-hand pair.

Foot edge

A simple foot edge was demonstrated on pages
32-3. To improve the appearance of this, having
worked to the right through two pairs in cst, twist
this pair (extreme right-hand one) once more
before putting in a pin and enclosing it with
another cst. To work a foot edge on the left, just
start with the third pair from the left and work to
the left through two pairs in cst. Make an extra
twist on the extreme left-hand pair, pin, and
enclose the pin with another cst.

Spider

The pricking (left) shows a hole in the centre of a diamond. The number of holes may vary, but there will always be an equal number of pairs of bobbins on either side of the centre. Twist the four pairs to give a total of three twists on each pair. Find the centre. *Work the pair from the left of centre towards the right in cs through all pairs. Work the next pair from the left to the right in cs through the same two pairs. * Place a pin between the centre pairs in the middle pinhole. Repeat from * to *. Twist all pairs three times. The finished spider should resemble the diagram on the right.

Cloth stitch block

Cloth stitch blocks may vary in size and shape but the way in which they are worked is always the same. Starting with the two pairs above a, work cs, twist weavers (in this case, the right-hand pair) twice and insert pin. Work weavers to the left through two pairs in cs, twist weavers twice, insert pin b. Work back through three pairs to c, and so on, adding one pair on each row until the widest point is reached (in this case h-j). Continue working but now leave out one pair at the end of each row until q (two pairs left). Work cs to cover last pin.

Diagonal finish

This is very much like the reverse of steps 3 and 4. When foot pins have been worked on both sides as far as o, and all centre work completed, one line of holes on each diagonal should remain unworked. Work the passive pair from each side (second pair in from the edge) to the centre through each pair in cst. Work two passive pairs together in cst. Work the edge pair from o to centre through each pair in hs, pin, hs, from u to z. Repeat for 4 to 9. Work these two pairs together at 10. Reef knot all pairs.

Tassel

Find the two centre pairs, hanging from 10, and bunch the remaining pairs each side of them. *The right-hand pair from 10 passes under the bunch to the right of it and back over. The left-hand pair from 10 passes over the bunch to the left of it and back under. These two pairs cross left over right in the centre. Repeat from *, pushing the working threads up really tightly. Work about 1.5cm-2cm. To secure the working threads, take one thread from each working pair and reef knot them. Repeat with the other two threads. Cut the tassel to the desired length.

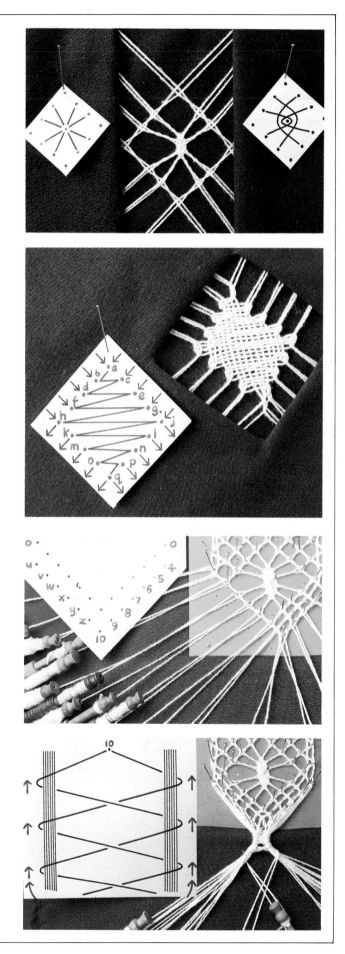

Bookmark

In addition to spiders, this attractive pattern makes use of alternating blocks of cloth stitch and half stitch, giving a pleasant appearance of light and shade.

Abbreviations

See page 33

You will need

For a bookmark, 17cm by 3.5cm

16 pairs of bobbins wound with DMC Fil à Dentelles
Heavyweight grossgrain ribbon the same width as the finished bookmark or a little wider and twice as long
Thread to match the ribbon

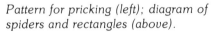

Making the lace

Make a pricking and copy the marking for spiders and rectangles on to it, using the numbers for easy reference.
Set up an imitation foot (step 3), using 14 pairs.
Set in the passive pairs (step 4).
Work the first cloth stitch block as shown in step 7 (rectangle marked A).
Work net stitches at pinholes x and y.
Work spider (step 6).
Work pinholes 2-10 (5, 8 and 10 are foot pins, the rest are net stitches).
Work block B in half stitch, reversing the direction of each row of stitches).
Work pinholes a-g (a and e are foot pins).
Work spider.

Work pinholes h-r (h, m, p and r are foot pins).
Work block A2 in cloth stitch.
Continue in this manner until the book mark is completed except for the final row of pins. Finish off as shown and make a tassel.

Mounting

Mount the lace on the ribbon, using lace thread. Make small back stitches over the bars of the foot edge at 1cm intervals.

Fold the ribbon in half and stitch the edges together, using matching thread.

Allow the corners to project beyond the lace to support the tassel. Stitch or fringe the bottom of the ribbon to finish.

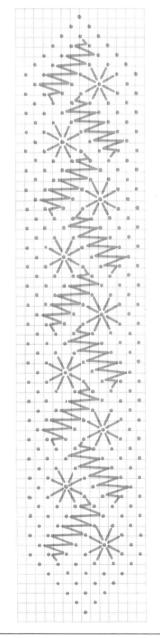

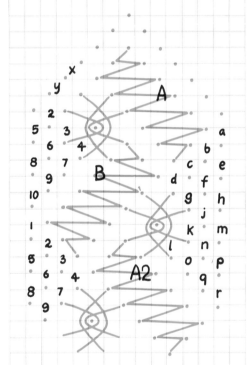

Pattern for pricking (left); diagram of spiders and rectangles (above).

Lavender bag

Although the Fir tree fan edging has been used here to decorate a lavender bag, the number of fans can easily be increased to make an edging for a handkerchief or a mat.

Abbreviations
See page 33

You will need
For a bag, 13cm by 13cm

9 pairs of bobbins wound with Bocken's linen thread No. 50
0.60 crochet hook
10cm of ivory evenweave linen, 35 threads to 2.5cm
One skein shaded stranded embroidery thread
Dried lavender

Making the lace
Copy the pattern as given on to graph paper and make a pricking (see page 32). It will be helpful to copy the markings for the fans as shown on all pattern repeats of the pricking, using a fine felt-tipped or ink pen. It is not necessary to copy the diagram numbers on to the pattern, merely use the diagram for easy reference.

To accommodate the corner it is necessary to start with pattern repeat II. Put a pin in each of the holes marked A, B, C, D, E, F and G in the bottom of pattern repeat I. Hang three pairs of bobbins on A and one each on B, C, D, E, F and G.
To work the foot and the net:
Pinhole 1 Work a foot pin as described in step 5.
Pinhole 2 Work a net stitch with left-

hand pair from 1 and pair from B (a net stitch is hs, pin, hs, as in Little Torchon fan, page 34).
Pinhole 3 Work a net stitch with the left-hand pair from 2 and the pair from C.
Pinholes 4 and 5 As pinhole 2, using the pairs from D and E in turn. Remove support pins A, B, C, D and E and carefully pull down the loops that are left.
Pinhole 6 As pinhole 1
Pinholes 7, 8 and 9 As pinhole 2, taking the left-hand pair from the previous pinhole and the pair from the pinhole in the row above.

Pinhole 10 As pinhole 1
Pinholes 11 and 12 As pinhole 2
Pinhole 13 As pinhole 1
Pinhole 14 As pinhole 2

Working the fan
Refer to step 1. Start at pinhole G (equals a) and follow the lines marked to show the path of the weavers, finishing at pinhole p. Remove support pin F after working pinhole e, and pull down loop.

Work next pattern repeat (III) in the same way.

The corner fan (IV) is worked as the other fans, but note that from g to x it is neater if there is an extra twist on the weavers after *every* stitch. Gradually turn the pillow as you work this section so that by the time w-x is being worked the pillow has been turned through an angle of 90 degrees. Finish the fan in the normal way.

Note that the next patch of net begins at pinhole 2.

Complete fan V then prepare to move the lace up (see page 33). The whole of the last pattern repeat should be pinned into pattern repeat I before continuing. Repeat for three more sides, then finish off the lace by joining the end to the begining. Cut threads close to knots.

Use the lace to trim a lavender bag, mounting it round the edge of the bag with lace thread, stitching into every foot pinhole.

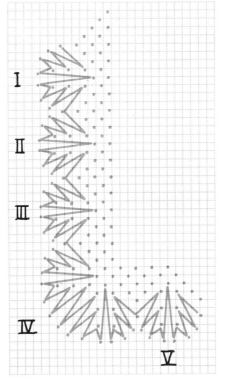

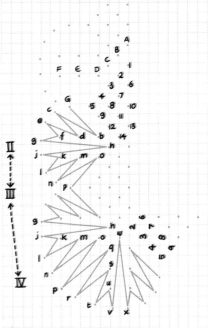

Correct order of working (above); pattern for pricking (left)

Chevron shapes

Lace is coming back into popularity as a household furnishing as people appreciate the beauty of a white or cream-coloured lace mat gracing a dark polished wood table.

Mats, coverings and trimmings of hand-made lace have always been used for furnishing and adorning church linen and some of the most beautiful altar frontals and chalice covers date back as far as the eighteenth century.

As a furnishing in ordinary homes, lace really came into its own during the Victorian era, with trimmings for blinds, mats for tables, runners on the piano, edgings for mantelpieces and many other uses. In many countries young girls would decorate the sheets

and pillowcases and table linen for their bottom drawer with edgings or insertions of hand-made lace.

In Edwardian times the vogue was for doileys, mats and tablecloth edgings, and today, as then, a lace mat adds grace and elegance to any setting.

Working a decorative edge

This can be achieved with a combination of passives. For the mat one of the simplest is shown, using two cs pairs of passives and one cst pair, with no foot edge. To work, there will be 3 pairs hanging between a and b, one at b, one at c and one at d. Pinhole 1: with pair from b cs through 2 pairs, tw weavers once, cst with last pair, tw weavers once, pin. Pinhole 2: weavers work cst through one pair, cs through 3 pairs, tw weavers twice, pin. Pinhole 3: as pinhole 1, but cs through one more pair. Pinhole 4: tw right-hand pair from pinhole 2 and work the net (hs, pin, hs — see page 33, pinholes 2, 3 and 5) with pair from d. Pinhole 5 as pinhole 2, 6 as 1, 7 as 4 and carry on.

Net stitches

The simplest net is hs, pin, hs, which is used in most basic Torchon lace. A firmer net may be made by working hs, pin, hs and tw (this has been done in the mat shown here because it provides a firmer background to the chevron pattern). A very firm net may be made by working cst, pin, cst. This net, which is called Dieppe Ground, is very useful if the thread is a little fine for the pattern chosen. It is a good idea to experiment with other combinations to see what effects can be achieved.

Zigzag trails

To keep a trail even (for example the chevron shapes in the mat) it is necessary to adjust the work at each change of direction. In a cloth stitch trail it is best to use a pinhole twice. The first time, use it normally, then when working back to it for the second time take out the pin and replace it in the hole supporting the weavers as if it had never been in before — the little loop from the previous weavers slides up between the pinhole and the previous one. Do not forget that a pair comes in when the hole is used for the first time, but is left out after it has been used for the second time.

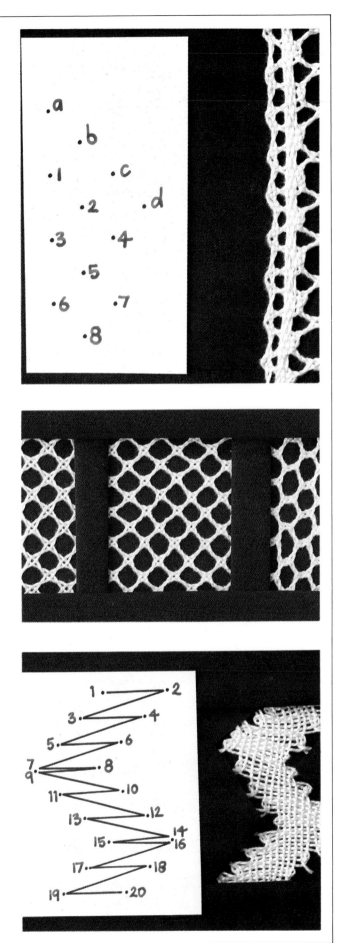

Zigzag trail in half stitch

The method used in step 3 is a little bulky for half stitch. Here it is better to change weavers when the chevron or trail changes direction. To do this, work to pinhole 8 or 14. Stick a pin in the hole in the normal way and leave. Take the outermost pair on the other side (left-hand pair at 7 or right-hand pair at 13) and use as new weavers. The threads run diagonally in hs, so this method leaves no holes here but would not work with cs.

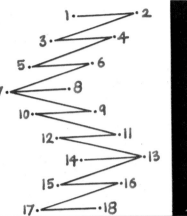

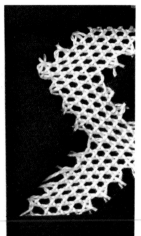

Finishing weavers and passives

After joining, a firmer finish than that shown on page 37 can be achieved as follows. Leave the ends long enough to be threaded into a sewing needle. When the lace is off the pillow, study the ends.

Passive threads should be darned a very short way, following the line along which they have travelled (in other words vertically). Outermost weavers can be darned upwards into the existing work in the same way, the threads being concealed within the weave of the cs.

Remaining threads

All other pairs should be stroked down to lie in line along the row of reef knots. Thread the topmost thread into a needle. *Make two small oversewing stitches round the other threads and the existing lace. Remove the two or three uppermost threads. Repeat from * all along the line, ensuring that the 'roll' is never thicker than about four threads. Finish with an extra oversewing stitch and cut all ends close to the work. There is now an obvious right and wrong side to the work, but the finish is very firm and will withstand far more laundering than if the threads had been cut close to the knots.

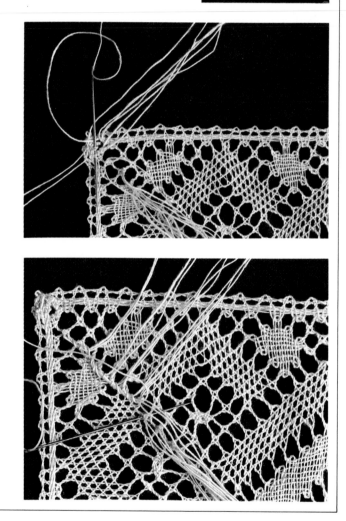

Square mat

This delightful little lace mat is worked with 30 pairs of bobbins, which may at first seem rather daunting. In fact, however, it is surprisingly easy to work with the higher number, the problems are only in the mind and the trick is to work methodically through the pattern. Keep the bobbins not in use away from the working area.

Abbreviations
See page 33

You will need
For a mat 13.5cm square, including the edge

30 pairs of bobbins wound with Bockens linen thread No. 50 in white or écru
0.60 crochet hook

Making the lace
Copy the pattern four times on to graph paper (10sq to 2.5cm) to make a square. Prick the whole mat in one to avoid moving the lace at all (see page 32). Copy all the markings on to at least the first quarter of the pricking. Use the diagram for reference.

Hang a pair on a pin in pinhole 1 and 3 pairs on support pins just above and to the right of it. Hang the other 26 pairs on support pins just above each pinhole on the diagonal (4, 6, 9 and so on) right down to the centre of the mat.

Pinhole 1 has weavers hanging from it.

Pinhole 2 Work weavers from 1 in cst through one pair and cs through 2 pairs, tw twice, pin.

Pinhole 3 Cs back from 2 through 2 pairs, tw weavers once, cst, tw once, pin.

Pinhole 4 As 2 but cs through one more pair (3 in total).

Pinhole 5 As 3 but cs through 3 pairs. Remove support pins.

Pinhole 6 Net stitch worked hs, pin hs and tw (see step 2) with pair from 4 and new pair. Remove support pin.

Pinhole 7 as pinhole 4, 8 as 5, 9 as 6, 10 as a net stitch, 11 as 4 and 12 as 5.

Work cs block A (see page 37).
Remove support pins after 6 pinholes have been worked and pull down loops.

Work pinholes 13 to 18 in the same

The diagram shows a quarter of the pattern and indicates the stitches worked

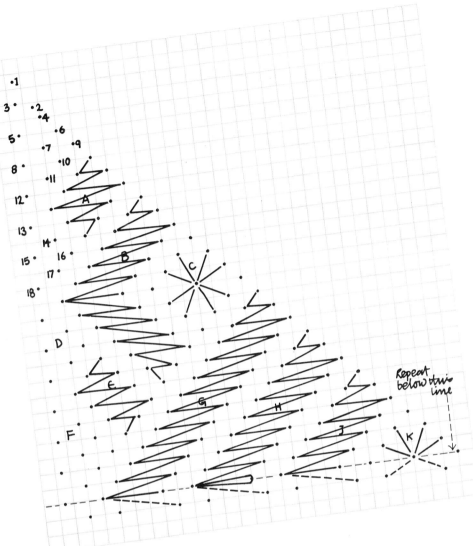

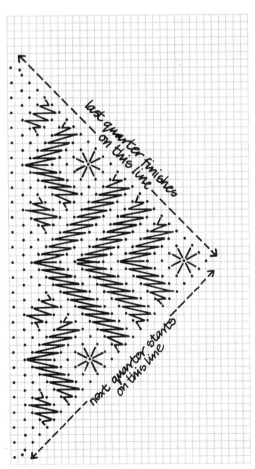

way as pinholes 5, 7, 8, 10, 11 and 12. Work first half of hs chevron B (starting as for cloth stitch block), then remove support pins after 6 pinholes have been worked and pull down loops.

Change weavers in the centre (step 4).

Work spider C (see page 37).

Remove support pins as the pairs are used for net stitches.

Complete hs chevron B.

Work net and edge (D) as pinholes 13 to 18 above.

Work cs block E as A.

Work net and edge (F) as pinholes 3 to 12.

Work first half of hs chevron G as B.

Work first half of cs chevron H.

Use pinhole twice at change of direction (step 3).

Remove support pins after 6 pinholes have been worked and pull down loops.

Work first half of hs chevron J.

Change weavers in the centre (step 4) and remove support pins as for chevron H.

Work spider K as C.

Complete hs chevron J.

Complete hs chevron H.

Complete hs chevron G.

The second part of the first quarter of the pattern is completed in the same manner as the first. The final 3 pinholes being worked like pinholes 3, 2 and 1. Turn the pillow through 90 degrees and it will be seen that all pairs are hanging from the completed quarter of the pattern ready to commence the second quarter.

Work the third and fourth quarters in the same way, then join the lace, finishing off as previously described.

The net in this pattern has 2 twists throughout between the pinholes. For the sake of uniformity and to make the pattern look neater, all pairs should have 2 twists on them when they pass from one section to another, for example from spider to chevron or from chevron to chevron.

Plaits and picots

Bedfordshire lace is as attractive as it is versatile, and less geometric in character than Torchon lace. It was very much in demand in the early Victorian era for collars and cuffs and is chosen by today's lacemakers for mats and medallions as well as simple or beautifully elaborate edgings.

The characteristics of the lace are reasonably easy to recognize. There is a fairly open appearance to the work and the different parts of the pattern are joined with what are often referred to as plaits. These use two pairs of bobbins, and therefore four threads. Picots are also used extensively — and add a delicate softening to the edges.

Another principal characteristic of the lace is that it has different names in different parts of the country — an oval, woven shape, somewhat like a laurel leaf. Two pairs of bobbins are used, with one thread weaving in and out of the other three in a figure-of-eight style. The shape of the leaf comes with the skill of the worker (for instructions see pages 48-9). Both the plaits and leaves are used to make edgings on their own or to join the cloth stitch or half stitch shapes which make up the body of the pattern.

Threads

Like Torchon lace, Bedfordshire lace can be made using either a fine or a coarser thread according to the use to which it will be put. In the early nineteenth century, Bedfordshire lace in its coarser forms was able to compete with machine-made lace in the same way as Torchon lace. Because of its durable qualities, linen thread was mostly used, otherwise cotton provided an alternative. Using very fine thread, Bedfordshire lace became one of the finest and most sought-after laces.

The Crown pattern

The simplest pattern in Bedfordshire lace is one called Ninepin, because nine pins are put in the pattern for every pattern repeat completed. This was the pattern which the children in the Bedfordshire lacemaking area learnt first when they started learning lace at school.

The Crown pattern, shown here, is a development of the Ninepin pattern, making an edging that adds delicate interest to a blouse.

Paperweight

The idea of making a piece of lace to go under a glass paperweight is a comparatively modern one. With some thought and a little ingenuity many simple edgings can be turned into circles suitable for this purpose. Alternatively, designs based on concentric circles drawn with a pair of compasses may be used. The glass paperweights are available from most lacemaking suppliers.

Two small circles of felt are needed to back the lace and it is very important to use a clear, all-purpose glue which will not show through.

Working the plait

Most people are used to plaiting with three strands. In bobbin lace, plaits are made with two pairs of bobbins and therefore have four strands. To make the plait, work a half stitch (see page 33) with the two pairs, then another half stitch and another, until the correct length is reached. Care must be taken over the tension so that the plait is neat and tight and lies flat.

Left-hand picot

Take the left-hand pair of the plait in the left hand and a pin in the right hand. Put the pin under the left-hand thread and draw the right-hand thread back to the left. Move the pin so that the point of the pin travels over the crossed threads, then turn it so that it goes down between the bobbins and up between the threads. Put the pin in the hole to the left of the plait so that a single thread forms the picot around the pin.

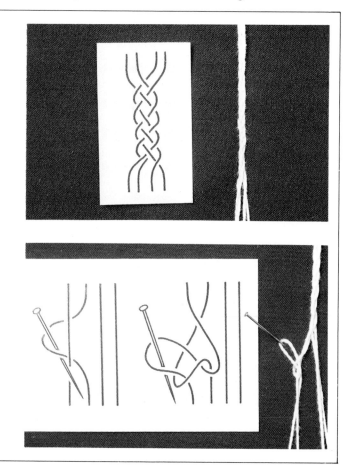

Right-hand picot

A right-hand picot is worked in exactly the same way as a left-hand picot, but reading right for left and left for right. The picot thus formed is rather like a little slip-knot around the pin, one which will not slacken with use and washing. This is just one of several types of picot but it is the best for this type of work. Where picots appear on either side of a plait, a half stitch must be worked between the picots or a hole will appear where not required.

Windmill

A 'windmill' is the name given to the crossing of two plaits or leaves. The pairs of bobbins are used as if they were single threads. Work the first two movements of a cloth stitch (see page 32). Place the pin in the hole in the centre of four pairs, then complete the cloth stitch. Pull the work up neatly around the pin.

Joining a plait to a trail

The weavers pass through all the passives in the usual way. The two pairs from the plait are each used as if they were single bobbins. Cloth stitch the weavers through these double threads. Twist the weavers twice and put in a pin *. Cloth stitch the weavers back through the double threads from the plait then continue as normal.

Removing pairs from a trail

If a plait or leaf joins a trail and is not to be left out for another plait or leaf, then the trail will thicken. To avoid this, pairs already in the trail must be removed from it. After joining the plait to the trail (up to * in step 5). ** remove one of the middle pairs of the existing passives by lifting it up and placing the bobbins at the back of the work, then work across the row. Repeat from ** for the next row, then continue in the usual way.

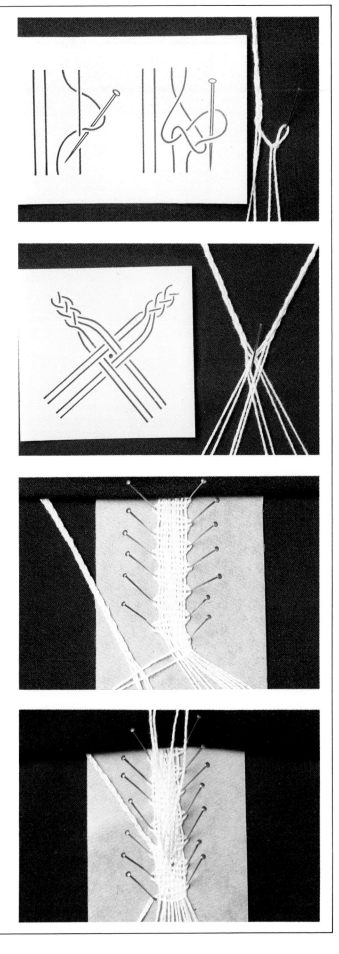

Lace edging

Providing it is handled with the care it deserves, this Bedfordshire lace edging should last for generations, adding the finishing touch to a whole succession of garments.

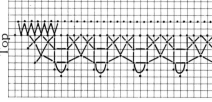

Abbreviations
See page 33

You will need
For an edging approximately 2cm deep which can be made to any length (each repeat is approximately 1.5cm long)

12 pairs of bobbins wound with DMC Brillanté d'Alsace No. 30

Making the lace
Copy the pattern on to graph paper with 10 squares to 2cm. Make a pricking (see page 32). If a longer length of lace is required make a second pricking and follow the instructions for moving up the lace as given on page 33. Copy all the markings for the plaits on to the whole of the pattern. The zigzags for the foot edge may be copied for just the first 2 or 3 centimetres to indicate the way of working.
Pinhole A Hang 2 pairs above the hole on support pins. Work hs, pin, hs and remove support pins.
Pinhole B Hang 4 pairs on support

pins above B. Work cst with left hand pair from A through these 4 pairs, twist weavers once and put in pin.
Pinhole C Cst with weavers through 5 pairs, twist weavers once. Put in pin in foot pin position (pin placed so that there are 2 pairs to right of it).
Pinhole D Hang 2 pairs open on a support pin (one outside the other) and join them to foot edge (step 5).
Pinhole E As pinhole C.
Pinhole F As pinhole B.
Pinhole G As pinhole C.
Remove all support pins and pull the loops down carefully.
Pinhole 1 Plait (step 1) the 2 pairs hanging from D until the pinhole is reached. Hang 2 pairs open on a support pin above the pinhole and work a windmill (step 4). Remove support pin. Plait the two right-hand pairs to H and leave and the 2 left-hand pairs to 2.
Pinhole 2 Hang 2 pairs open on a support pin above the pinhole and work a windmill. Remove the support pin. Plait the 2 right-hand pairs to 3 and the 2 left-hand pairs to 5.

Pinhole H As step 5.
Pinhole J As pinhole C.
Pinhole K As pinhole B.
Pinhole L As pinhole C.
Pinhole 3 Plait the 2 pairs from H and windmill with the plait from 2. Plait to 4 and M.
Pinhole M As pinhole H.
Pinhole 4 Plait the 2 pairs from M and windmill with plait from 3. Plait to 10 and 5.
Pinhole 5 Windmill with plaits from 2 and 4.
Plait to 9 and 6.
Pinhole 6 Picot (step 2), plait to 7.
Pinhole 7 Picot, plait to 8.
Pinhole 8 Picot, plait to 9.
Pinhole 9 Windmill with plaits from 5 and 8. Plait to 2 and 10.
Pinhole 10 Windmill with plaits from 4 and 9. Plait to 1 and D.
The first pattern repeat is now completed. Work until the desired length is achieved. If the ends of the lace are to be inserted into the seam of a garment, then just reef knot each pair for security. If a complete circle is required, the end should be joined to the beginning as shown in step 2 on page 35.

Paperweight

A clear glass paperweight is an excellent way to display a small, delicate piece of lace and it makes a lovely and unusual gift.

Abbreviations
See page 33

You will need
For a lace motif approximately 5cm in diameter to fit a paperweight 7cm in diameter

22 pairs of bobbins wound with DMC Brillanté d'Alsace No. 40
Scraps of felt for mounting
Paperweight approximately 7cm in diameter
Clear all-purpose glue (Uhu is ideal as it does not discolour the lace)

Making the lace
Trace or photocopy the pattern and make a pricking (see page 32). Transfer all the markings on to the pricking.
Pinhole A Put a pin in this hole and hang one pair on it. Hang 8 pairs from support pins set behind and between A and B.
Pinhole B With pair from A cst through one pair and cs through 7

pairs, twist weavers and put in pin.

Pinhole C Cs through 7 pairs, twist weavers once and cst through edge pair. Twist weavers once and put in pin.

Pinhole D Cst through one pair, cs through 5 pairs. Twist weavers twice and put in pin.

Pinhole E Cs through 5 pairs, twist weavers once, cst through one pair. Twist weavers once and put in pin. Remove support pins and carefully pull down loops.

Pinhole F As pinhole D.

Pinhole G As pinhole E.

Continue until pinhole U is worked. Work back to outside edge at A2.

Pinhole 1 With the 2 pairs hanging at B plait (step 1) to pinhole 1 and work a left-hand picot (step 2).

Pinhole 2 Plait to pinhole 2, hang 2 pairs open (one outside the other) on a support pin behind 2 and work windmill (step 4).

Remove support pin.

Pinhole 3 With the 2 left-hand pairs from 2, plait to 3 and work left-hand picot.

Pinhole 4 Hs, work right-hand picot (step 3), plait to 7.

Pinhole 5 With the 2 right-hand pairs from 2, plait to 5, make a right-hand picot and plait to e.

Pinhole a Hang a pair on a pin in this hole and 8 pairs on support pins

Both prickings are shown full size so that they can be traced or photocopied.

set behind and between pinholes a and b.

Pinhole b Cs through 3 pairs, twist weavers twice, cs through 5 pairs, twist weavers twice and put in pin.

Pinhole c Cs through 5 pairs, twist weavers twice, cs through 3 pairs, twist weavers twice and put in pin.

Pinhole d Cs through 3 pairs, twist weavers twice, cs through 3 pairs, twist weavers twice and put in pin.

Pinhole e As pinhole d, then join plait to trail (step 5).

Remove support pins and carefully pull down loops.

Pinhole f As pinhole d.

Pinhole g As pinhole d.

Continue until pinhole m is reached, bringing in plaits and working outside ring as before.

Pinhole b2 Before working from a2 to b2 hang 2 more pairs on support pins behind and to the right of b2. Work to pinhole m2.

With 2 pairs from b plait to X, working right-hand and left-hand picots as required.

Repeat with 2 pairs from b2.

Pinhole X Work a windmill with 2 pairs from b and 2 pairs from b2. Plait the 2 sets of 2 pairs from X to b3 and b4, working right-hand and left-hand picots as required.

Work inner and outer rings until b3 is reached. Then work on to remove 2 pairs from the trail (step 6).

Continue until the whole medallion is completed, removing 2 more pairs from the inner trail where necessary. Push the pins flat and turn the pillow as required.

To finish off, work from U8 back to A and hook in weavers to loop of pinhole A (see page 35). Work weavers across to B and repeat. Reef knot weavers. Repeat for pinholes a and b. Make a final plait to 2 and hook in each pair in turn to this pinhole. Reef knot each pair. Cut all ends long enough to thread into a needle and remove from pillow.

Mounting

Select a piece of felt a little larger than the paperweight. Mount the medallion on this by darning all loose ends through to the wrong side.

Using clear, all-purpose glue, make a thin line of glue all around the raised rim of the paperweight. Centre the paperweight carefully over the lace and press it down on the felt. Leave it until the glue is dry.

Glue another piece of felt carefully on to the back to cover all the loose ends. When this is dry carefully trim away excess felt around the paperweight.

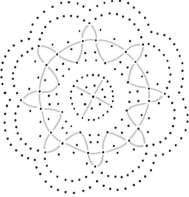

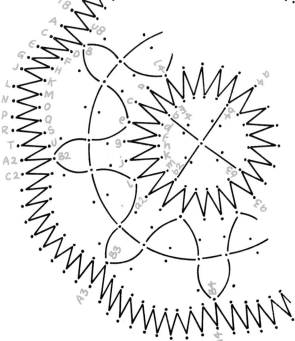

Leaves and tallies

Leaves are characteristic of Bedfordshire lace and can either be used to make edgings on their own or may be incorporated into designs including cloth stitch or half stitch shapes.

Bedfordshire lace is extremely versatile and can be used either for comparatively simple edgings or for very complex and beautiful designs. Few, if indeed any lacemakers, can hope to emulate the brilliant inventiveness of the eminent nineteenth-century designer Thomas Lester, but Bedfordshire lace remains popular with modern designers and is a technique well worth learning and exploring.

Materials
For a mat, like the one featured here, it is generally best to choose a good quality linen fabric and to make the lace with a linen thread. This should wash and wear much better than cotton and, if treated with reasonable care, should last much longer. Since any lace takes a fair amount of time to make, it is commonsense to be prepared to spend just a little bit extra on materials in order to create something which is durable.

Leaves
The main characteristic of Bedfordshire lace is the leaf shape. These leaves have many different names, such as woven plaits, wheat ears or almonds, depending on the part of the country in which they have been made. Leaves and plaits are found in all sorts of combinations in different samples of Bedfordshire lace and always enhance the appearance of a pattern. Leaves are not easy to work and a lacemaker is well advised to practise quite a number of them in a long line before putting them into a pattern for the first time.

Tallies
The Bedfordshire lace shape has a close cousin which has a blunt-ended form. This often occurs in the fillings in Honiton lace, where it is referred to as a leadwork. This is because it is supposed to remind the lacemaker of the little diamond-shaped leaded lights, so

popular in the windows of the cottages in Devon. These square-ended shapes also occur in Buckinghamshire lace where they are also referred to as tallies, long dots or even cucumbers. Dealers often call the shape a *point d'esprit*, adopting the French name.

Lace care

Any mat that is in constant use is likely to need fairly frequent laundering. Consequently linen thread, which will stand up to this sort of treatment, is strongly recommended. When laundering any lace that is hand-made, whether new or old, treat it with care. It should be hand-washed in a mild, hand-hot detergent solution. Choose a brand that does not have any optical brightener or blue-whitener in it, nor any bleach. When washed, rinse it very thoroughly then carefully pull it into shape whilst it is dripping wet. Most items can be spread out carefully on the side of the bath or on flat tiles in the bathroom and then left to dry naturally.

When the lace is removed it will have a crisp and fresh feel and will not need starching. *Do not* iron if there is any way this can be avoided, and if it is absolutely essential to do so, iron only the fabric to which the lace is attached. Ironing seems to squash the life out of a piece of lace. Treated well, lace should last a very long time. Store away in a cupboard out of direct sunlight.

To prevent discoloration most lace-makers store their white laces, either flat or rolled, between layers of blue tissue paper (not white).

Starting a tally

A tally uses two pairs of bobbins. Take the second bobbin in from the left and pass it over the bobbin immediately to the right of it and under the one beyond. Return, passing the weaving thread over the right-hand bobbin, under the centre one, and over and back under the one on the far left. A full figure-of-eight movement has thus been completed.

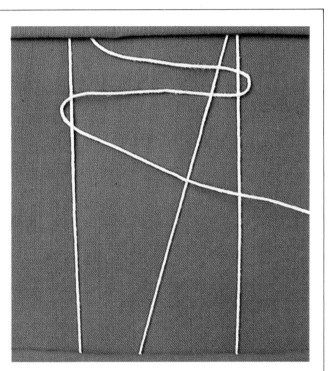

Completing a tally

A tally is completed when a sufficient number of figure-of-eight movements have been worked to give the required shape, whether this be long, square or wide. It is worth noting that the square shapes are the easiest ones to begin with. Care must be taken with the tension of the tally so that the sides remain straight, taut and parallel with each other.

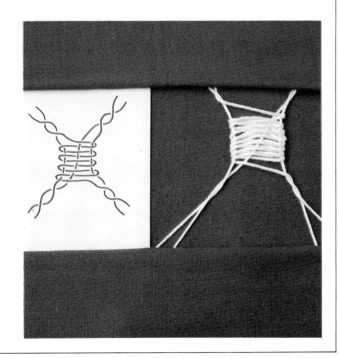

Starting a leaf

A leaf is very much like a tally, the main difference being its shape. If the worker can make tallies, then leaves should present few problems. The leaf, also made with two pairs of bobbins, starts with a cloth stitch to draw all four threads together, then the weaving is done just as in the tally. Take care over the shaping so that it ends like an oval laurel leaf.

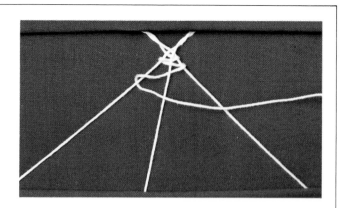

Completing a leaf

Once the shaping of the leaf is completed, it is finished off in much the same way as it was begun, namely by using a cloth stitch to draw the four threads together. To help the shaping of the leaf, the worker should try to think of it as the rather angular shape shown in the diagram. It should then be possible to make the threads flow to make the curved shape required.

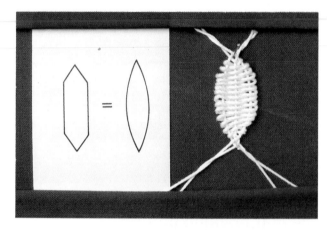

A six-pair crossing

Handling the pairs as if they were single threads, pass the pair to the right of centre under the pair to the right of it. Pass the pair to the left of centre over the pair to the left of it. Cross the two centre pairs left over right. Pass the pair to the right of centre under the pair to the right of it and over the pair beyond. Pass the pair to the left of centre over the pair to the left of it and under the pair beyond.

Finishing

Stick a pin in the hole in the centre of the work so far completed. Pass the pair to the right of centre under the pair to the right of it. Pass the pair to the left of centre over the pair to the left of it. Cross the two centre pairs left over right. Pass the pair to the right of centre under the pair to the right of it. Pass the pair to the left of centre over the pair to the left of it. Pull all threads carefully into position around the pin.

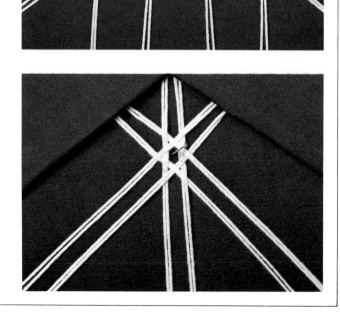

Bedfordshire lace mat

This little mat with its linen centre should wash and wear well since it is made with a durable linen thread and the outer edge of the work is quite firm.

Abbreviations
See page 33

You will need
For a mat, approximately 12cm in diameter.

About 20 pairs of bobbins wound with Campbells linen thread No. 100 (if you prefer cotton, use DMC Brillanté d'Alsace No. 30)
Small piece of linen for the centre of the mat

Preparation
Photocopy or trace the pricking and transfer it to a piece of pricking card. Add all the markings to the pricking with a fine black waterproof pen.

There is no diagram for this pattern

Lace mat pricking pattern

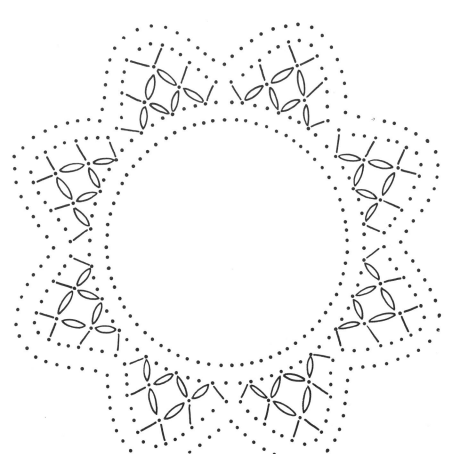

as, apart from the leaves, there are no very difficult new techniques to be learned. As usual, work round the pattern in an anti-clockwise direction so that the foot edge will be on the right-hand side.

Making the lace
Select a foot pinhole (one on the extreme right of the pattern) opposite the narrowest part of the pattern and hang two pairs of bobbins on support pins just behind this point. Work hs, pin in the foot pinhole, hs and remove the support pins so that the pairs drop down around this pinhole. With the left pair work in cs through a number of passive pairs — about four to seven pairs. It is worth experimenting here to see how many pairs you consider make an attractive foot edge. Making a proper foot-side edge, work until the line for the first plait joins the foot-side trail.

Now start on the outer trail. Hang a pair of bobbins on a pin in the pinhole on the outside edge in the extreme angle of the curve. These will be the weavers. In the same way as for the foot-side trail, decide how many pairs of passives will make an attractive trail, but always work the outermost pair in cst for firmness. Work across to the first pinhole. It will be noted that a plait must be joined in at this point. Two pairs are added as at the beginning of the Crown edging (see page 46) and are left for use as a plaited pair.

Carry on working down the outer trail, adding two lots of two pairs for the two subsequent plaits.

Stop when the widest point of the pattern is reached. Work the three plaits. The two pairs from the first plait are joined to the foot-side trail in the same manner as the Crown edging and then make a leaf to the point at which they windmill with the two pairs from the second plait.

Both groups of two pairs then make leaves to the point at which they join the next stage of the work. The left-hand pairs windmill with the pairs from the third plait and the right-hand pairs join the foot-side trail.

Complete the whole patch of plaits, leaves and windmills. It will be noted that the three plaits have nowhere to go except into the outer trail until they are used for the next patch of plaits, leaves and windmills. This means that the trail is thicker by up to six extra pairs for this section. Consequently care must be taken over the tension in this part of the work so that it does not bubble, and care must be taken over the original number of pairs to be used in this trail so that it looks neither too sparse nor too crowded.

When the mat is completed the trails should be finished in the same way as the medallion (see page 49) except that instead of making reef knots you should darn the ends into the beginning of the work for firmness and neatness.

Mounting
To mount the mat, mark lightly on the linen fabric a circle exactly the same size as that of the centre of the lace mat and use this line as a stitching guide, but do not cut out. Stitch the lace to the linen, using punch stitch or buttonhole stitch and the same thread as that which was used to make the lace. Trim the edge of the fabric closely on the wrong side and lightly oversew the raw edge to prevent it from fraying. Finish the work by pressing the linen carefully on the wrong side.

Chapter 3

Tatting

Tatting produces a beautiful open lace, made by repeating a few simple movements using a shuttle and thread — in much the same way as a hand-stitched button loop is made. Despite its filigree effect, however, tatted lace is surprisingly strong and therefore eminently suitable for many home furnishings.

The instructions given on the following pages are in the form of lessons with built-in projects. These progress from very easy to more intricate, and end with helpful suggestions on how to create your own simple tatting designs.

The basic skills can be learned quickly while making attractive lampshade trims, appliqué motifs and pretty edgings for clothes, followed by more advanced techniques for making stunningly intricate placemats and tablecloths, even jewellery — a stylish beaded choker, and an exquisite pair of lacy mitts that a bride would simply adore. You'll find something here to suit all levels of skill and the most demanding taste.

Edgings

**Tatting is a simple yet delicate lace with an infinite number of uses.
Tatted rings and picots make a pretty edging to collars and cuffs,
whether on everyday clothes or on wedding dresses.**

Only one knot, or stitch, is used in tatting, and this is built up in series to form the delicate rings and chains which combine to make up the design. Tatting may consist entirely of rings or entirely of chains but most designs incorporate both, and occasionally, picots.

Equipment
Shuttles and hooks Modern tatting shuttles are usually about 6cm to 8cm long. Many have a central spool which can be removed for winding.

Some shuttles have a small hook built into them while in other cases a separate hook is often supplied by the maker.

It is sometimes possible to find old shuttles in antique shops. Early shuttles made in bone, tortoiseshell or ivory can be very attractive. They are frequently larger than the modern shuttle which, although perfect for lightweight threads, cannot always hold a useful length of thick thread.

Threads These should be smooth and evenly spun. Threads which give or stretch are not suitable. Mercerized crochet cottons are commonly used. The heavier pearl cottons are suitable for beginners but have the disadvantage that, being thick, they soon fill the small shuttles.

For practice pieces, very coarse threads such as string or cord in a light colour can be very useful. Wind the thread into a figure-of-eight and secure with a rubber band for a makeshift shuttle. Otherwise, a newcomer to tatting should fill a medium size shuttle and begin as follows.

To begin tatting
Wind the thread on to the shuttle. Take care not to overload the shuttle so that the thread protrudes over the edges, in which case it might get dirty. Holding the shuttle in the right hand, unwind about 45cm of thread and grip the end between the thumb and forefinger of the left hand. Wind the thread around the outstretched fingers of the left hand to form a ring.

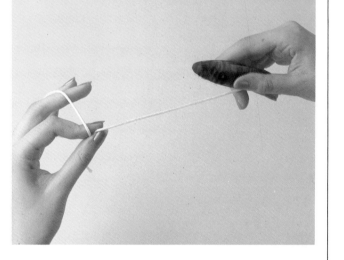

Looping the thread
Lay the shuttle thread in a loop over the top of the hand and pass the shuttle up through both the ring and the loop. It is easiest to keep the third and fourth fingers of the left hand over the ring and curled in towards the palm.

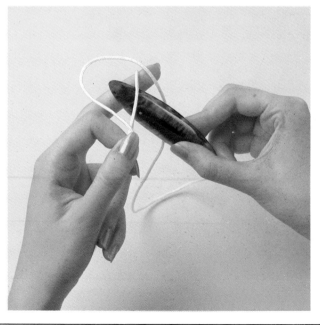

Transferring the loop

The shuttle is now looped on the ring and has to be inverted so that the loop is formed by the ring thread and runs along the shuttle thread. To do this, pull the shuttle to the right while lowering the second finger of the left hand. (It does not matter if the ring slips off the finger as it will still be held by the others.)

Completing the transfer

As you pull the shuttle thread, making sure that the loop is still slack, the loop will automatically be inverted. Raise the lowered second finger so that the loop can gently be tightened. Hold this loop (a half stitch) with the thumb and forefinger to prevent it from slipping back. It should now be possible to slide the half stitch along the shuttle thread, making the ring larger or smaller.

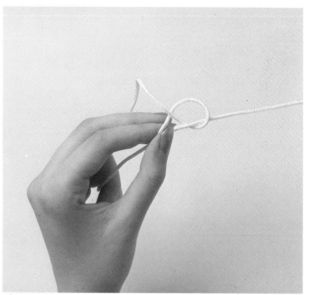

The second half of the double stitch

Pass the shuttle downwards through the ring and over the shuttle thread. Transfer the loop so that it runs along the shuttle thread as explained. Tighten and position it next to the first half stitch, completing the basic double stitch. Practise a series of double stitches, making sure that they all run easily along the shuttle thread. As the ring thread becomes used up, stretch the fingers of the left hand to enlarge the ring.

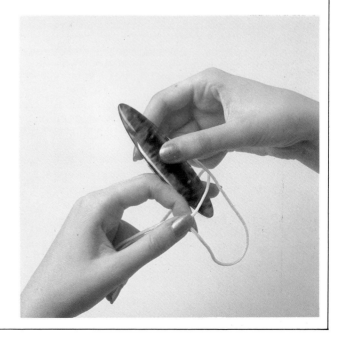

To make a ring

When a series of double stitches has been worked, slip the work off the left hand while retaining the grip with the thumb and forefinger, and gently pull the shuttle thread to draw in the ring. It should close completely. If it does not do so, then at some stage the transfer of a loop has been omitted or incorrectly carried out. Tatting will not unravel, but stitches can be loosened and unpicked with the hook.

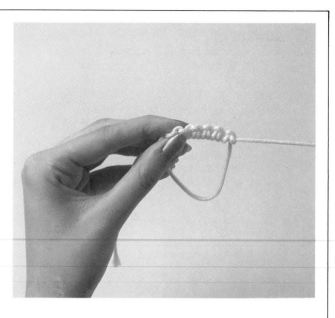

To make a picot

After completing the first half of a double stitch, leave a small space of about 6mm between this half stitch and the last complete stitch. Make the second half of the stitch and tighten this into position. Push the double stitch which has just been made back to meet the first. The space will form a picot.

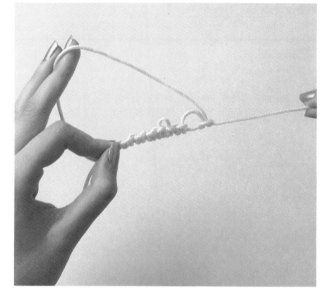

To join two rings

Work a ring of four double stitches, picot, four double stitches, picot, four double stitches, picot, four double stitches. Close the ring. Start a second ring close by with four double stitches. Join to the last picot of the first ring by inserting the hook through this picot, drawing a loop of thread from the ring around the left hand and pulling it out sufficiently to insert the shuttle.

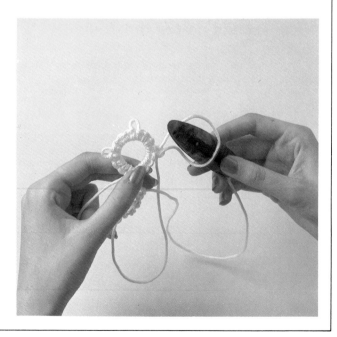

Completing the join

Pass the shuttle through the loop and then tighten the loop. It must slide on the shuttle thread and it takes the place of the first half stitch. Follow it with a second half stitch, which secures the join, and complete the ring with three double stitches, picot, four double stitches, picot, four double stitches, close. The double stitch carrying a picot counts as the first in the series between the join and the next picot.

Abbreviations

The following abbreviations are used in tatting patterns:

A, B, C   the letters of the alphabet are used to identify individual rings or chains
ch(s)   chain(s)
cl   close
ds   double stitch
hs   half stitch
JK   Josephine knot

(to be explained later in the chapter)
p   picot
r(s)   ring(s)
RW   reverse work (this is when work is turned upside down in the hands so that it faces the other way)
smp   small picot
sp   space

Tatted lace edgings

Shown worked in a lightweight cotton as trimmings for a doll's clothes, these edgings could also be used to trim nightwear or underwear or, worked in slightly heavier cotton, they could give a finishing touch to children's or adults' clothes.

Abbreviations
See page 57

You will need
For edgings, 1cm, 1.5cm and 2cm wide

No. 60 mercerized crochet cotton (to make lightweight trim) or
No. 3 or 5 pearl or No. 20 crochet cotton (to work a heavier lace)
Tatting shuttle
Tatting hook

Edging 1
Ring A of 4ds, p, 2ds, p, 4ds, close.
*Ring B of 4ds, join to last picot of ring A, (2ds, p) 6 times, 4ds, close.
Ring C of 4ds, join to last picot of ring B, 2ds, p, 4ds, close.
Leave a space of about 1cm.
Ring A of 4ds, join to last picot of ring C, 2ds, p, 4ds, close.
Repeat from * for length required.
Attach to fabric by overcasting the space thread.

Edging 2
Ring A of (3ds, p) 3 times, 3ds, close, RW.
*Ring B of 4ds, p, 4ds, close, RW.
Ring A of 3ds, join to last picot of previous ring A, (3ds, p) twice, 3ds, close, RW.
Ring C of 4ds, join to picot of ring B, (2ds, p) 7 times, 2ds, close, RW.
Ring A of 3ds, join to last picot of previous ring A, (3ds, p) twice, 3ds, close, RW.
Repeat from * for length required.
Attach to fabric by overcasting the free picots of rings A.

Edging 3
Ring A of 4ds, p, (2ds, p) 7 times, 4ds, close, RW.
Ring B of 4ds, p, (2ds, p) 7 times, 4ds, close, RW.
*Ring C of 3ds, join to last picot of ring A, 3ds, p, 3ds, close, RW.
Ring D of 3ds, join to last picot of ring B, 3ds, p, 3ds, close, RW.
Ring A of 4ds, join to picot of ring C, (2ds, p) 7 times, 4ds, close, RW.

Ring B of 4ds, join to picot of ring D, (2ds, p) 7 times, 4ds, close, RW.
Repeat from * for length required.
Attach to fabric by overcasting the centre of the trimming.

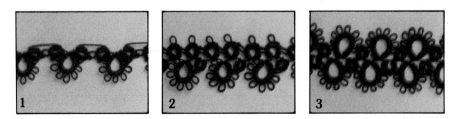

All three of these tatted edgings are relatively easy to make and will give ideal practice in the basic technique of tatting

Working in rounds

Tatting makes delicate lace edgings for clothes but it can also be worked in consecutive rounds, rather like crochet, to make elegant mats and covers formed entirely of tatted lace.

The basic tatted ring is a natural geometric shape which repeats to form flower-like shapes. A ring may be any size, but large ones will tend to distort from a perfect circular shape, becoming oval or pear-shaped. Often this distortion can be an advantage to the design, as can be seen in the rosette centres of the table mats featured here, where the large rings forming the central rosette tend to point towards the centre of the group.

A group of consecutive rings may be of any size. A small group of just three rings makes the classic 'clover' shape, while four rings suggest a square and a larger group makes the 'rosette'.

These basic shapes may be repeated and joined together to make an all-over pattern or used as a centre motif with concentric rounds of tatting added to make a more interesting design. Each additional round of tatting is joined to the preceding round in the same way that rings are joined to one another.

Josephine knots

Minute tatted rings made from a small number of stitches become knot-like. Josephine knots (sometimes called Josephine rings or Josephine picots) are tiny knot-like rings worked with half stitches instead of the usual double stitches. The name first appeared in France and may perhaps have been given in honour of Empress Josephine.

Picots

Rings of all sizes, whether made individually and finished off or worked in groups, can be used to build up a colourful collage 'bouquet' and the skillful use of picots can greatly add to the interest and variety of such a bouquet. Try varying the number and lengths of the picots. Some rings can be left bare while others are heavily embellished with picots as a contrast.

Rings with a plentiful supply of picots resemble little eyes complete with lashes, which accounts for the old Italian name for tatting — *occhi* (eyes). Picots used for decoration can be elongated to any length desired and can also be graduated in length, but picots needed for joins should always

be as small and unobtrusive as possible, indeed they need only be large enough to allow the hook to be inserted. Long picots twist badly if washed and are therefore only suitable for work which is intended to be mounted or protected in some way and used solely as decoration.

Gigantic picots can be cut and frayed out to form a fringe. Collage bouquets of rings, with or without picots, can be quickly mounted on card, using a spray adhesive, or they can be sewn on to lampshades or curtains. Make them in colours picked out from your interior scheme for a coordinated look.

Working a rosette

A rosette is a series of connected rings with no spaces between them, forming a natural flower shape, the final ring being joined to the first picot of the first ring. To avoid a twisted picot, fold the first ring forwards to lie over and in front of the unfinished final ring. Insert the hook into the picot and draw the left-hand thread through into a loop, completing the join in the usual way. When the rings are finished, tie the ends to connect the centre.

Tying the shuttle thread

To avoid having to cut the shuttle thread and join it at another place, take the thread (at the back of the work) from the centre of the rosette to the picot connecting the first and last rings. Insert the hook into the picot, catch the thread and pull it into a loop, then pass the shuttle through the loop and adjust the knot. This method can be used to take the shuttle thread to any free picot, where it will be in position for further work.

Josephine knots

A small ring of half stitches is called a Josephine knot (JK). Either the first or the second half stitch may be used, but the latter is quicker to work. Hold the thread in the usual way as for a ring, work a series of half stitches, about six or eight, and close the ring tightly to form a knot. Josephine knots are sometimes used to connect parts of a design. They do not normally carry picots.

Overlapping the joins

New threads are joined in by overlapping sufficient
new and old thread to encircle the hand and then
working three or four double stitches with a
double thickness before dropping the old thread
and continuing with the new. The overlap should
be planned at the beginning of a ring and the ends
should only be trimmed after the ring has been
securely closed. To keep the appearance of the
pattern, the number of stitches may have to be
decreased where there is a double thickness of
thread. Do not work picots with a double thread.

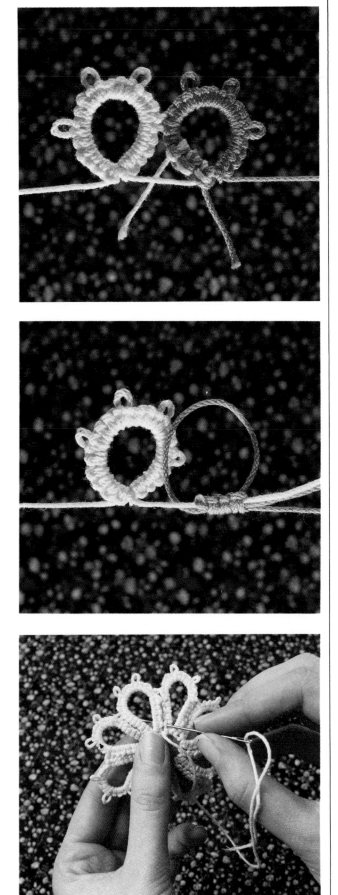

To hide a knot

Sometimes a mistake occurs which will not unpick
and which has to be cut out, leaving an end which
is too short for an overlap join. In this case, tie the
old and new threads at the beginning of a ring
and run these ends along the shuttle thread so
that they lie inside a series of double stitches. Use
the hook to pull the ends through as each half
stitch is formed but before it is tightened. This
method is very neat, especially if the ends are
trimmed to different lengths.

To darn in ends

Final ends should not be cut off short as they will
work loose during wear. Leave ends of sufficient
length to thread a needle and darn them into the
tatting. Ideally, it is best to run them inside the
double stitches but in practice this can be difficult
and it is usually easier to stab-stitch neatly through
the heads of several stitches. Very coarse yarns
can be divided into strands and each strand
darned in separately.

Pressing

Tatting intended for regular wear and washing can be pressed under a damp cloth but to display an ornate piece at its best do not iron. Instead, pin the wet tatting to an ironing board or similar surface, stretching it well, and leave the piece until it is completely dry before removing the pins. Pin accurately and make sure that all the picots are pulled into place.

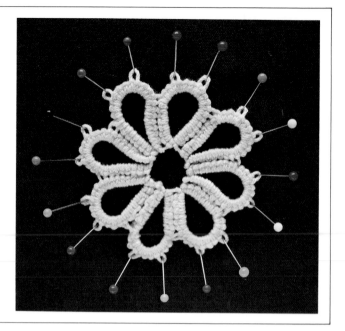

Placemat and glass mat

The pattern given here has been used to make a place mat and a glass mat, but it is very simple to adjust the size simply by adding or subtracting rounds of tatting.

Abbreviations
See page 57

You will need
For a place mat, approximately 23cm in diameter and a glass mat, approximately 13cm in diameter.

No. 5 pearl cotton
Tatting shuttle
Tatting hook

Placemat
Ring of 8ds, p, (4ds, p) 3 times, 8ds, close.

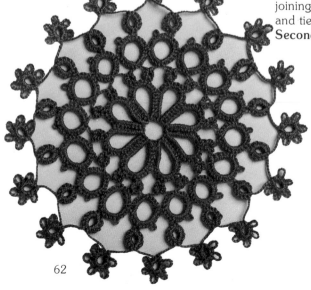

*Ring of 8ds, join to last picot of previous ring, (4ds, p) 3 times, 8ds, close. Repeat from * 6 times more, omitting last picot of last ring and joining it instead to first picot of first ring.
Tie the threads to join the centre of the rosette, tying the shuttle thread to the picot between the first and last rings. Then tie the shuttle thread to the second picot of the first ring ready to begin the first round.
First round JK of 4hs, join to picot to which the thread is tied, 4hs, close, RW. Leave a space of 3mm.
Ring of 6ds, p, (4ds, p) 3 times, 6ds, close, RW. Space of 3mm.
*JK of 4hs, join to next free picot on rosette, 4hs, close, RW. Space of 3mm.
Ring of 6ds, join to last picot on previous ring, (4ds, p) 3 times, 6ds, close, RW. Space of 3mm.
Repeat from * all round the rosette, joining the last ring to the first. Cut and tie thread to first JK.
Second and following rounds JK of

4hs, join to any free picot of first round, 4hs, close. Leave a space of 6mm.
*JK of 4hs, join to next picot on previous round, 4hs, close. Space of 6mm.
Repeat from * all round work, and continue in concentric rounds, joining all the following JKs to the spaces instead of to picots.
As the mat gradually emerges, enlarge the spaces between the JKs. Continue for eight rounds or for the size required.
Cut thread.
Final round Ring of 6ds, join to any space of previous round, 6ds, close, RW. Space of 12mm.
*Ring of (2ds, p) 5 times, 2ds, close, RW. Space of 12mm.
Ring of 6ds, join to next space of previous round, 6ds, close, RW. Space of 12mm.
Repeat from * all round. Cut and tie ends.

Glass mat
Work centre rosette and first round as for place mat.
Final round Ring of 6ds, join to first picot of any ring of previous round, 6ds, close. RW. Space of 12mm.
*Ring of (2ds, p) 5 times, 2ds, close, RW. Space of 12mm.
Ring of 6ds, join to first picot of next ring of previous round, 6ds, close, RW. Space of 12mm.
Repeat from * all round. Cut and tie ends.
Damp each mat, pin out and leave to dry.

Worked in coloured threads such as strong pastels and deep neutrals, tatted mats make an interesting contrast when placed on to a highly polished table or a crisp white linen cloth

Working with chains

Although tatting is built up from one basic stitch, the effects which can be produced are very varied, ranging from dainty edgings for clothes to rich, heavy lace for mats and coverings.

Once the chain has been mastered, it is possible to create a vast range of tatted designs, using chains and half-stitch chains to link rosettes or to form intricate looped patterns.

Designs
Many modern tatting designs feature both rings and chains in their composition, and the trend is towards the use of colour rather than all-white work. Although it is easy to use two different colours for the two threads needed for tatting with rings plus chains, care should be taken in their choice, as sometimes two opposing colours can detract from the linear shapes which make up a tatting design.

If you can devote only a limited amount of time to your tatting, pieces made up from motifs are an ideal choice. Single motifs can be joined into manageable units which can then be combined at a later stage.

To make a chain

Two threads are needed, one on the shuttle and one wound in a ball. Different colours may be used. Knot both together for practising and hold the knot firmly between the first finger and thumb of the left hand. The ball thread goes over the back of the hand and around the fourth finger. There should be about 25cm of thread unwound from the shuttle. The ball thread now takes the place of the ring thread and double stitches are worked in the usual way in series to form a chain.

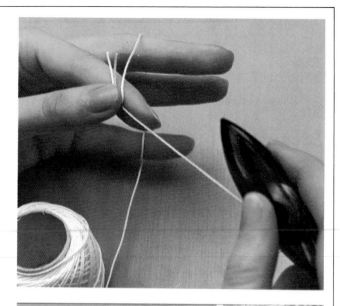

Chains and rings

Join chains to chains or rings by the method given on pages 56-7 for joining rings. If a chain is to be followed by a ring, drop the ball thread from the left hand and use the shuttle thread on its own. If, after working a ring, the pattern requires a chain, pick up the ball thread on the left hand. Begin each ring or chain as close as possible to the preceding ring or chain unless otherwise directed. Work is usually reversed at each changeover.

Avoiding knots

When winding a shuttle, do not cut it from the ball to begin a project. However, if the threads are already cut apart and providing both are the same colour, a knot can be avoided by unwinding some of the shuttle thread, transferring this to the ball, and making an overlap join, as shown on page 61, when the break in the ball thread is later reached.

To join motifs

Repeating motifs are joined while they are being made and not after completion. They are joined by the same method given for joining two rings on pages 56-7. It is sometimes hard to decide which parts of the design should be joined, and frequent reference must be made to the illustration. If a join has been forgotten, the picots can usually be sewn together with a needle, and this should not be noticeable in the finished work.

Using two shuttles

The ball thread can be wound on a second shuttle, with the thread still being placed around the fourth finger of the left hand. It is helpful if the two shuttles are of a different colour or design. A second shuttle is needed in order to work Josephine knots on a chain, as the knots are in this case worked with the 'ball' thread and not with the main shuttle thread.

Half stitch chains

Work a larger number of half stitches (use the second half stitch for speed) in series as a chain, and the heads of the stitches will spiral round the shuttle thread in an atractive way. This technique is not traditional, but it is worth using in experimental work, especially with heavy threads. Spiral chains are particularly useful as a basis for tatted necklaces or as the stems of flower sprays.

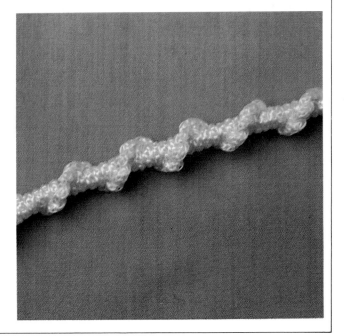

Table centre

A table centre for the great occasion. The six-sided motif is not difficult to work — concentration is needed in joining the component parts of the design but the heavy richness of the tatting, and the beautiful snowflake pattern, makes it well worth the effort.

Abbreviations
See page 57

You will need
For a table centre, 46cm in diameter (Individual motifs measure 8cm across)

Four 20g balls of No. 10 mercerized crochet cotton

First motif
Work this initial motif as follows:
Ring A of 6ds, p, (3ds, p) twice, 6ds, p, 6ds, close, RW.
Chain A of 8ds.

Ring of 8ds, p, 4ds, p, 4ds, close.
*Ring C of 4ds, p, 4ds, p, 8ds, close, RW.
Chain B of 8ds, join to last picot of Ring A, RW.
Chain C of 10ds, join of last picot of Ring C, (4ds, p) 3 times, 10ds, RW.
Ring A of 6ds, join to next picot of previous Ring A, (3ds, p) twice, 6ds, p, 6ds, close, RW.
Chain A of 8ds.
Ring B of 8ds, join to last picot of Chain C, 4ds, p, 4ds, close.
Repeat from * 3 times more. Work Ring C, Chain B, Chain C as before.
Ring A of 6ds, join to next picot of previous Ring A, 3ds, p, 3ds, join to first picot of first Ring A, 6ds, p, 6ds, close, RW.
Work Chain A, Ring B, Ring C, Chain B as before.
Chain C of 10ds, join to Ring C, (4ds, p) twice, 4ds, join to first Ring B, 10ds, cut and tie threads to first Ring A to complete motif.

Second motif
Work as first motif till Chain B is completed.
Chain C of 10ds, join to last picot of Ring C, 4ds, p, 4ds, join to corresponding picot on any Chain C on first motif, 4ds, p, 10ds, RW.
Work Ring A, Chain A as usual.
Ring B of 8ds, join to last picot of Chain C, 4ds, join to corresponding ring on first motif, 4ds, close.
Ring C of 4ds, join to corresponding ring on first motif, 4ds, p, 8ds, close, RW.
Chain B as usual.
Chain C of 10ds, join to last picot of Ring C, 4ds, join to corresponding picot on Chain C of first motif, (4ds, p) twice, 10ds, RW.
Complete second motif as for first.
All motifs are joined in this manner. Thirty-seven are needed to complete the mat, joined as shown. When the table centre is finished, press it under a damp cloth.

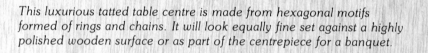

This luxurious tatted table centre is made from hexagonal motifs formed of rings and chains. It will look equally fine set against a highly polished wooden surface or as part of the centrepiece for a banquet.

Stitch variations

The basic technique of tatting is very easy to master and the craft offers great scope for those who wish to experiment with and create their own designs for pretty lace edgings.

Once the double stitch has been mastered, tatting is a simple process, rings with or without chains being used with picots to form beautiful traditional lace work. However, there are several ways in which tatting can be varied, not only in the approach to design but in the skills and techniques used. The craft is still developing and there is no reason why newer, more original methods should not be evolved.

The double stitch is made up of two halves and different effects can be produced by varying the sequence of the two halves. A repeated half stitch can be used to produce a chain on which the heads or edges of the stitches form a spiral effect (see page 68). This spiral edge can be exploited further by varying the combination of the two halves of the double stitch. For instance, calling the first half stitch 'a' and the second 'b', work 3a, 3b, 3a, 3b and so on, or 5a, 5b, 5a, 5b, or even 3a, 5b, 3a, 5b: the resulting spiral edge will continually change direction, producing a wavy effect. It is better to work this in a fairly thick thread so that the spiral patterns can clearly be seen in the finished design.

Old books on tatting refer to these combinations of half stitches as 'sets', so the method is not new, but has fallen out of general use. However, one of the most talented modern British designer/tatters, Elgiva Nicholls, has exploited this technique and calls it the node switch or node stitch, since the change of the wavy edge results in a protruding knob or node, even without added picots.

Varied and interesting designs can be worked entirely in node stitch or it can be combined with the more common tatted rings and chains formed from the ordinary complete double stitch. Whether it is used on its own or with the double stitch, it is a useful addition to the repertoire of any tatter and is well worth bearing in mind when you are planning a design.

Picots

Some ways of varying ornamental picots by elongating them or cutting and fraying them have already been mentioned (see pages 59-60), but there are other, non-traditional ways of using picots. One of the advantages of node stitch is that it makes it possible to place picots on both sides of a chain, something which is not possible in ordinary tatting. Another picot variation is the twisted bar (see page 68), made by twisting a long picot before using it for a join. Alternatively, a bead can be threaded on a long picot before it is used as a join. The traditional way of working chains with beads is to thread them on to the ball thread beforehand.

In designs made of rings, beads can also be threaded on the shuttle thread and slid up into place between rings, but this method is inconvenient in practice, as the beads may be too bulky on the shuttle and catch during work. Beaded picots provide a neat and simple solution to this problem.

Beads

When choosing beads, make sure that they relate to the strength of the design and are not so heavy that the work will be pulled out of shape. If they are to be threaded on to picots, make sure that the holes are large enough to take a double thickness of the selected thread. (See Adding beads to picots.)

Design

Once the basic stitch and its variations have been learned, it is very easy, and very good practice, to start working out a few simple designs of your own. Make small experimental scraps, trying out different threads and combinations of rings, chains, picot effects and node stitch variations.

Whenever you have worked a small sample which you feel might come in useful as part of a larger design, staple it to a sheet of paper and put it in a ring binder for future reference together with the instructions. When, at a later date, you wish to build the sample piece into a design, it may help to look at it through a magnifying glass in order to count the stitches.

A node stitch chain

Calling the first half stitch 'a' and the second half
'b' (see page 55 for half stitches), hold the shuttle
and ball thread in the usual way and work *4a,
4b. Repeat from * for the required length. These
are 'sets' of four. It is important to count
accurately and not to lose the sequence, otherwise
the effect will be spoilt. The centre chain shows
the reverse side of the work. The lower chain
shows sets of four with picots (4a, picot, 4b, picot
and so on).

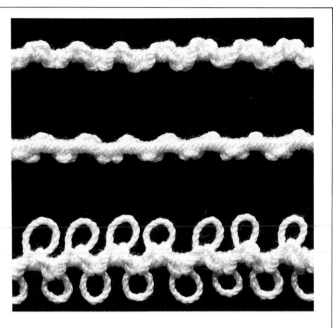

A node stitch ring

Hold the shuttle thread in the usual way to form a
ring and work 4a, 4b six times. Again, it is
important to count accurately to avoid losing the
sequence. Close the ring and, if necessary, gently
push the heads of the stitches to the front of the
work. Picots can be added and the size of the
rings may be varied. Entire ring and chain designs
can be made in this way or it is possible to work
sets in conjunction with the usual double stitch.

Gauging the length of picots

If a pattern contains several long picots of equal
length, it is worthwhile measuring these accurately
rather than leaving it to guesswork. Cut a small
piece of card as a gauge. The length of the card is
immaterial but the width should be twice the
length of the required picot. Once the gauge is
cut, it is a simple matter to insert it between the
two threads while making a picot.

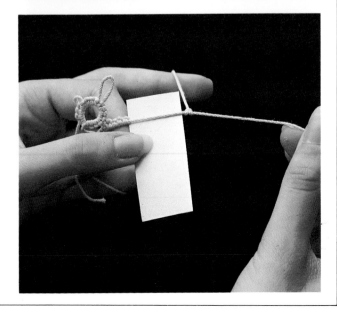

Adding beads to picots

Make a picot of a sufficient length to carry the bead and also to allow room for the hook to be inserted. When the picot join is reached, loop a short piece of bead wire or 5 amp fuse wire through the picot and slip the bead over this and on to the picot. Insert the hook, remove the wire and complete the join in the usual way. It is best to experiment before beginning a major project in order to get the width of the gauge exactly right.

To work a bar

Make an extra-long picot to be used as a join. When this join is subsequently reached, twist the picot with the fingers or with the hook then insert the hook to catch the left-hand thread and complete the join in the ordinary way. For a good tension, always give the same number of twists on repeating units of a pattern, and twist in the same direction throughout. 'Bars' can be used to join rings or chains.

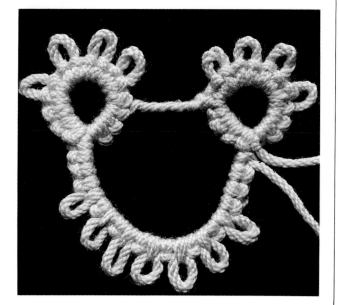

Rubbings

Once the basic stitches have been learnt, start making your own designs. An easy way to do this is to make rubbings. Hold a sample of tatting against a window pane with a piece of thin white paper over the tatting, then make a rubbing using the side of a crayon. Make a second rubbing next to the first, experimenting until you have a good combination. Note which picots will be needed for joins (rubbings of edging 2, page 58, are here placed back-to-back).

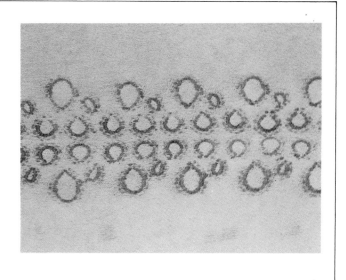

Building up designs

Edgings can often be put back-to-back to make a wider trimming. An easy way to judge whether this will work is to use your collection of samples and rubbings. This is also helpful in showing how a single motif can be repeated to make many different patterns. Take a rubbing from the sample motif and make a second rubbing next to it. Continue in this way, experimenting with different ways of connecting the motifs. The motif shown on page 63 is here re-arranged in a different design.

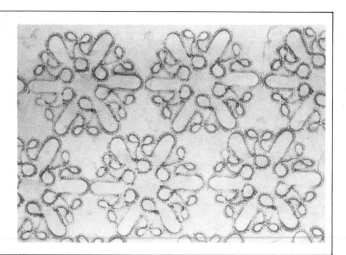

Tatted choker

This tatted choker is an attractive accessory and can easily be adapted — leave out the centre motif to make a narrower necklace for a higher neckline or add an extra repeat at either end to make a pretty collar.

Abbreviations

See page 57

You will need

For a choker, 30cm long by 11cm deep at the centre front

One 20g ball of Coats Crochet Cotton No. 10
17 beads, each approximately 7mm long
Small strip of card for a gauge
Short length of bead wire
Ribbon for ties

Main row

*Ring A of 7ds, p, 7ds, close. RW.
Chain A of 7s, long p (length of bead), 7ds.
Ring B of 7ds, p, 7ds, close. RW.
Chain B of 7ds, join to picot of Ring A, 7ds, RW.
Ring C of 7ds, join to picot of Ring B, 7ds, close. RW.
Chain C of 7ds, p, 5ds, p, 7ds, RW.
Ring D of 7ds, join to picot of Ring B, 7ds, close. RW.
Chain D of 7ds, p, 7ds, RW.
Ring E of 7ds, join to picot of Ring B, 7ds, close.
Chain E of 7ds, long p, 7ds, RW.
Ring F of 7ds, join to picot of Chain D, 7ds, close.
Ring G of 7ds, p, 7ds, close. RW.
Chain F of 7ds, RW.
Ring H of 7ds, join to picot of Ring G, 7ds, p, 7ds, close. RW.

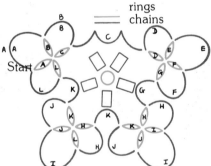

rings
chains

Chain G of 7ds. RW.
Ring I of 7ds, join to last picot of Ring H, 7ds, close.
Repeat from * 5 times more, ending with the last repeat at Ring F.
Finish off.

Inner row

Ring A of 4ds, p, 4ds, join with a bead to 1st long picot of main row, 4ds, p, 4ds, close. RW. Space of 2mm.
Ring B of 3ds, p, 3ds, p, 3ds, p, 3ds, close. RW. Space of 2mm.
*Ring A of 4ds, join to last picot of previous Ring A, 4ds, p, 4ds, p, 4ds, close. RW. Space of 2mm.
Ring B of 3ds, join to last picot of

previous Ring B, 3ds, p, 3ds, p, 3ds, close. RW. Space of 2mm.
Ring A as last Ring A.
Ring B as last Ring B.
Ring A of 4ds, join to last picot of previous Ring A, 4ds, join with a bead to next long picot on main row, 4ds, p, 4ds, close. RW. Space of 2mm.
Ring B as before.
Repeat from * all along, joining every 3rd Ring A to the main row with a bead. Finish off after final Ring A has been worked.

Centre front motif

Centre ring of 2ds, long p (length of bead), (4ds, long p) 4 times, 2ds, close. Finish off and start again with:
Ring A of 7ds, p, 7ds, close. RW.
Chain A of 7ds, p, 5ds, join to 2nd picot of Chain C of 3rd scallop of main row counting from the left, 7ds. RW.
Ring B of 7ds, join to picot of Ring A, 7ds, close. RW.
Chain B of 7ds, join to picot joining Chain D and Ring F of main row, 7ds. RW.
Ring C as Ring B, but do not RW.
Chain C of 7ds, join to any picot of centre ring with a bead, 7ds, join by shuttle thread to main row at junction of Rings G and H, 7ds, join by shuttle thread to main row at junction of Rings H and I, 7ds, join to next picot on centre ring with a bead, 7ds.

Outer row

With the choker upside-down in the hands, join the shuttle thread to the beginning of the main row, to the left-hand side, and work Node stitch as follows: * Chain of (4a, 4b) 5 times (= 5 sets), join with shuttle thread to 1st picot of Chain C, 4 sets,

join similarly to next picot of Chain C, 5 sets, join to junction of Chain D and Ring F, 4 sets, join to junction of Rings G and H, 4 sets, join to junction of Rings H and I, 4 sets, join to junction of Ring A and Chain B. Repeat from * once more.
Continue chain with 5 sets, join to 1st picot of Chain C, 4 sets, join to junction of Chain C of main row and chain E of motif, 2 sets, join to next picot of Chain E of motif, 5 sets, join to junction of Chains F and H, 5 sets, join to 1st picot of Chain I, 4 sets, join to next picot of Chain I, 5 sets. RW. Ring of 7ds, join to junction of Chains J and H at lower centre of motif, 7ds, close. RW. Complete remainder of row to match. Finish off.

Finishing
Pin the choker to a flat surface then damp the tatting with a spray and leave it until it is completely dry. Thread narrow ribbon through the rings at the back to tie.
Ring D as Ring A.
Chain D of 7ds, join to main row at junction of Ring A and Chain B, 7ds. RW.
Ring E of 7ds, join to Ring D, 7ds, close. RW.
Chain E of 7ds, join to 1st picot of Chain C of 4th scallop of main row, 5ds, p, 7ds, RW.
Ring F as Ring E.
Chain F of 7ds, p, 7ds, RW.
Ring G as Ring E, but do not RW.
Chain G of 7ds, join with a bead to next long picot of centre ring, 7ds.
*Ring H as Ring A.
Chain H of 7ds, join to Chain F, 7ds. RW.
Ring I of 7ds, join to Ring H, 7ds, close. RW.
Chain I of 7ds, p, 5ds, p, 7ds. RW.
Ring J as Ring I.
Chain J as Chain F.
Ring K as Ring I, but do not RW.
Chain K as Chain G.
Repeat from * once more.
Ring L of 7ds, join to Ring A, 7ds, close.
RW.
Chain L of 7ds, join to chain J, 7ds. Finish off, joining ends to beginning of motif.

Both the Victorian-style choker and the lace trimming at the top and bottom of the lampshade combine 'ordinary' (double stitch) tatting with node stitch sets and beads.

Lampshade edging

Tatting edgings, with or without beads, make the perfect trimming for a lampshade.

Abbreviations
See page 57

You will need
For an edging, about 2cm wide without the beads

Two 20g balls of Coats Mercer Crochet No. 10, one in pale green and one in cream
Faceted drop beads
Round green beads
Round, faceted pink beads
Small strip of card for a gauge
Short length of bead wire
Fabric adhesive (optional)

Note The lampshade shown here, which is 16cm in diameter at the bottom, used eight beads of each type for the trimming.

The lower edge
Using green, work Ring A of 8ds, p, 4ds, p, 4ds, close. Ring B of 4ds, join to last picot of Ring A, 6ds, p, 6ds, p, 4ds, close. Ring C of 4ds, join to last picot of Ring B, 4ds, p, 8ds, close. RW.
Using cream as the ball thread, make a chain of (4a, 4b) twice, long p (the length of the bead — the beads are attached in the sequence faceted, pink, green), (4a, 4b) 3 times, long p, (4a, 4b) twice. RW.
* Ring A of 8ds, join to last picot of Ring C, 4ds, p, 4ds, close.
Ring B as before. Ring C as before. RW.
Chain of (4a, 4b) twice, join with bead to last picot of previous chain, (4a, 4b) 3 times, long p, (4a, 4b) twice. RW.
Repeat from * for length required.
Join final Ring C to first Ring A at beginning, and omit last picot of final chain, joining instead to first long picot with a bead. Finish off.

Upper edge
Work the rings as given for the lower edge. For each chain work (4a, 4b) six times, omitting picots and beads.

Making up
Damp each edging to shrink it slightly and when dry stretch it to an exact fit for the lampshade. Attach the edgings with adhesive or sew them in place with matching cotton.

Speedy method

Once you have mastered the basic method of tatting and the ways in which the appearance of the finished work can be varied using sequences of stitches and threads of different colours, you may like to improve your speed.

There are various ways of handling the shuttle in order to produce the initial loop which forms the basic double stitch of tatting. The easiest method for a beginner who wishes to learn from written instructions is given on pages 54–55, but this is not the quickest method, and once you have mastered the first technique it is a good idea to experiment with the speedier method of handling the shuttle given overleaf. It should, however, be pointed out that the most difficult stage in tatting, that of transferring the loop from the shuttle thread to the thread around the left hand, is common to all methods.

The steps give the first half stitch before the second half, since this is the logical sequence, but in fact you will find it easier to learn the second half stitch first. It is important that the shuttle is held exactly in the way shown and that the thread leads from it in just the correct position. With practice, the passes can be performed extremely quickly, the speed contributing to the necessary tension which enables the

thread to snap into place. As with all methods, care must be given to the transfer of the loop.

Another point to bear in mind with this method is the choice of shuttle. When working quickly it is easy to drop the shuttle by accident, so be sure to pick one that does not unwind as it falls. A shuttle with open points is not suitable, and most tatters will find that a plain shuttle without any hook or projection is best for practising this quicker method.

As with all new techniques, it may take a little while to perfect this method of tatting and it is a little more difficult than the method already shown, but the resulting increase in speed will more than justify any time and trouble spent practising.

Threads

It is not always easy to obtain the exact colour of thread which one would like when planning a colour scheme in tatting. If the required colour is not available in the range of mercerized

Embroidery cottons are available in a wide range of colours and are ideal for making tatted motifs and braids to decorate a plain sweater or cardigan.

crochet cottons which are so popular for tatting, extend the search to include pearl cottons, which are available in various thicknesses, or embroidery thread (silk or cotton), where a much greater range of colours is available.

These threads, being loosely twisted, do not stand up to wear and tear to the same extent as mercerized crochet cottons, but the softer threads are perfectly suitable for appliqué work, where the background fabric helps to give the support and strength which the finished work would otherwise lack.

Artificially constructed threads are also worth bearing in mind. For example, a glossy rayon thread will often combine admirably with a matt thread of a similar colour and tone. However, some synthetic threads have a springy quality which causes ends or picots to loosen, but again they are perfectly suitable for tatting appliqué.

Alternatively you may like to try dyeing thread to your own requirements. A soft, loosely-spun thread, especially a cotton, usually takes the dye better than a hard, tightly-spun one. Dyeing is best done before the tatting is worked, or the colour tends to be stronger where the piece is more solid. The old-fashioned way to tint finished white tatting, giving it an 'antique' look, is to dip it in tea, or black coffee, which works equally well. Each gives its own slightly different écru tint, which will lighten and eventually disappear with laundering.

Mixing colours
When working a ring-and-chain design in contrasting colours, it is usual to have one colour on the shuttle and the contrast colour on the ball thread, but when working all-ring designs in colour it is often useful to have more than one shuttle — a separate shuttle for each colour. Alternatively, if the design permits, you can use a single shuttle, re-winding it at each colour change. The trim on the lavender-coloured sweater featured here requires two shuttles because the colours are continually alternating.

Finishing off
One great advantage of using tatting for appliqué is that the ends need not be finished off in the normal way (see page 61), but can be taken through the background fabric and used to sew the trimming into position.

Holding the shuttle
Leave approximately 45cm of thread unwound and hold the shuttle in the right hand, exactly as shown in the picture, so that the thread protrudes from the back of the shuttle and from the end nearest the right hand. Grip the end of the thread with the thumb and forefinger of the left hand and wind it around the outstretched fingers of the left hand to form a ring. Keep this ring taut.

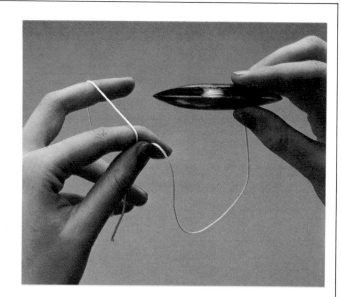

The first half stitch
Take the shuttle thread between the third and fourth fingers of the right hand, so that it catches on the tip of the fourth finger. Keeping the shuttle thread taut, pass the shuttle under the shuttle thread and through the ring around the left hand, pushing it upwards against the ring thread, which is also taut.

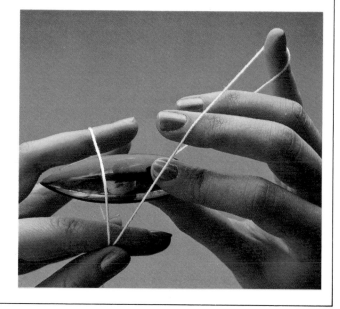

Making the pass

The tension of the pushing action should pass the ring thread over the top of the shuttle and back underneath it in one movement, all without the finger or thumb being removed from the shuttle. Being careful to keep the same grip on the shuttle, take it backwards under the shuttle thread, allowing the thread to drop from the little finger and then from the rest of the hand.

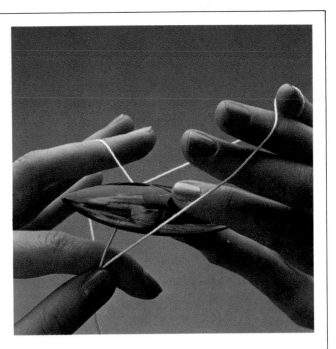

Transferring the loop

The shuttle thread is now looped on the ring thread and has to be transferred so that the ring thread is looped on the shuttle thread. Keep the loop loose and transfer it by jerking the shuttle to the right, while at the same time slackening the ring thread by gently lowering the second finger of the left hand.

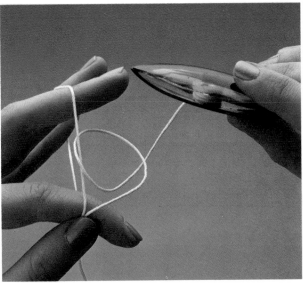

Completing the first half stitch

The ring thread is now looped on the shuttle thread. Raise the lowered second finger so that the loop can be gently tightened to form the first half of the double stitch. Hold it with the thumb and forefinger to prevent it from slipping back. It should slide easily on the shuttle thread.

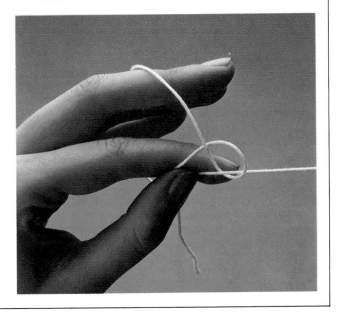

The second half stitch

Pass the shuttle to the left, pressing it down on top of the taut ring thread. Pressure from the shuttle should make the ring thread, underneath, snap back over the top of the shuttle. Withdraw the shuttle without removing either finger or thumb. The shuttle thread is now looped on the ring thread.

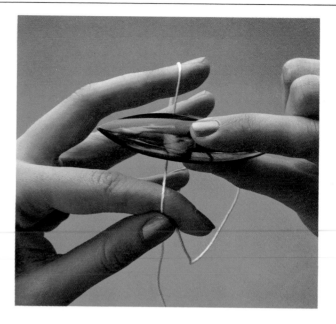

Completing the stitch

Repeat step 4 to transfer this loop as before. Tighten it to form the second half of the double stitch and hold it next to the first, so that the two form a pair, making a double stitch. The completed double stitch should run easily on the shuttle thread.

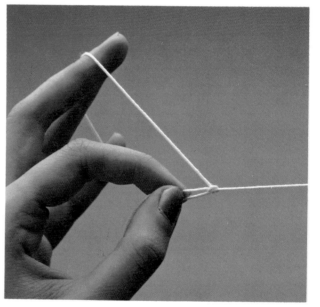

Tatting appliqué

Make a multi-coloured flower spray or a tatted braid with separate motifs to add to a plain sweater, or devise your own motifs as described on pages 68-70.

Abbreviations
See page 57

You will need
For the flower spray (yellow sweater) approximately 18cm long:

Pearl cotton No. 5, one ball or skein each of green and lilac (for the leaf fronds and the large flower)
Coats Mercer Crochet No. 10 in purple (for the small and medium-sized flowers)
1 tatting shuttle

For the motifs and braid (lavender sweater) 2.5cm and 2cm deep respectively:

1 ball of Twilley's Lystwist
1 ball of Coats Mercer Crochet No. 10
2 tatting shuttles

Flower spray

Large flower
Using pearl cotton, make Ring A of 9ds, p, (2ds, p) 4 times, 9ds.
Ring B of 9ds, join to last picot of previous ring, (2ds, p) 4 times, 9ds.
Repeat Ring B 7 times, making 9

petals altogether. Finish off, leaving an end for sewing.

Medium-sized flower (make 2)
Using Mercer Crochet cotton, work as for large flower but make 7 petals only.

Small flower (make 2)
Using Mercer Crochet cotton, make Ring A of 7ds, p, (2ds, p) 4 times, 7ds.
Ring B of 7ds, join to last picot of previous Ring, (2ds, p) 4 times, 7ds.
Repeat Ring B twice, making 4 petals altogether. Finish off as before.

Leaf frond (make 3)
Using pearl cotton, make *Ring A of

9ds, p, 5ds.
Ring B of 5ds, join to picot of Ring A, 9ds.
Join thread to junction of rings (i.e. with thread at back of work, insert hook into picot, draw through loop, pass the shuttle through this loop and adjust knot).
Repeat from * once more.
Ring C of 7ds, p, 7ds. Finish off as before.

To make the spray

Pin the individual pieces in a spray formation on the front of the sweater as shown in the diagram, taking all ends through to the back of the fabric. Sew it into position.

Motifs

To make the small motifs on the lavender-colour sweater, wind shuttle A with Mercer Crochet cotton and shuttle B with Lystwist. Tie both ends together, leaving ends long enough for sewing.
Using shuttle A, make Ring A of (2ds, p) 6 times, 7ds.
Ring B of 7ds, join to last picot of Ring A, (2ds, p) 5 times, 2ds.
Using shuttle B, tie thread to junction of Rings A and B (i.e. with thread at back of work, insert hook into picot, draw through a loop, pass the shuttle through this loop and adjust knot).
Ring C of (2ds, p) 7 times, 2ds.

Finish off, leaving ends for sewing. Make as many motifs as required (9 were used for the lavender sweater featured here).

Braid

Prepare shuttles as for motifs.
*Using shuttle A, make Ring A of (2ds, p) 6 times, 7ds.
Using shuttle B, make Ring B of 7ds, join to last picot of Ring A, (2ds, p) 5 times, 2ds.
Take both shuttle threads as one and tie to junction of Rings A and B. Repeat from * as needed.
Finish off, leaving ends for sewing.

To attach motifs and braid

Pin motifs and braid in position on the garment and take all the ends through to the back of the fabric, using a hook. Sew in place.

Tatted net

Thread left unworked between rings of tatting can be used for a diamond-shaped mesh which forms tatted net. The rings can be varied in size, and are often worked on a more solid piece of tatting.

The technique of tatting net is an easy one, but care is needed to make sure that the spaces of unworked thread which form the mesh are all approximately the same length. For a special effort such as an exhibition project, each space can be measured with a cardboard gauge.

Combining rings and chains

Each ring or chain should start as close as possible to the preceding ring or chain. Work is usually reversed when changing from rings to chains or vice versa. This means that the front of a ring and the back of a chain are on the same side of the work. There is therefore no right or wrong side in

tatting with rings and chains combined.

When sewing or tying in loose ends, keep them to one side of the work which will become the reverse side.

Tying the shuttle thread

Normally, all rings and chains in tatting are connected using the method for joining rings, as shown on page 56, and the method for joining chains where the thread around the left hand is looped through a picot. However, pattern directions will occasionally specify that the right-hand thread (the shuttle thread) should be used to connect a chain, to avoid an unwanted twist. This join is called a 'tied' to distinguish it from the usual join.

Victorian-style lacy mittens

These lovely Victorian-style mittens are ideal for a bride as a pretty foil for her ring and bouquet of flowers.

Abbreviations

See page 57

You will need

For a pair of mittens, medium size

One 20g ball of Coats Crochet Cotton No. 20
Tatting shuttle
Fine hook
Short length of shirring elastic

To work the basic net

1 Using only the shuttle thread, begin a ring and work 3 double stitches (or the number required to form half a ring), join to picot, then work an equal number of double stitches to complete the ring, closing it as usual.

2 Leave a space, gripping with the thumbnail to judge the position of the second ring, and work half a ring again, join to the next picot on the strip of tatting and complete the ring as before. Repeat all along.

3 For the second row, join the ring to the space thread, inserting the hook into the loop made by the thread as though inserting into a picot.

4 Repeat step 3 all along, leaving a similar space between each ring.

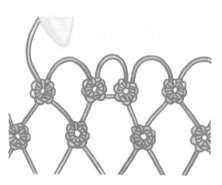

5 To increase, work an extra ring, joining it to the same space thread as the previous ring.

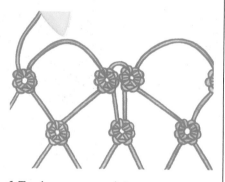

6 To decrease, work two consecutive rings together, omitting the space between them.

The cuff

Using shuttle thread only.
Ring A 9ds, p, (4ds, p) twice, 9ds.
*Ring B 9ds, join to last picot of previous ring, (2ds, p) 4 times, 9ds.
Ring C As ring B.
Ring D As ring B.
Ring E 9ds, join to last picot of ring D, (4ds, p) twice, 9ds. Reverse work.
Using ball and shuttle threads:
Chain A 9ds, p, 9ds, tie the shuttle thread to last picot of ring E, 9ds, p, 9ds. Reverse work.
Using shuttle thread only:
Ring A 9ds, join in junction of ring E and chain A, 4ds, join to centre picot of ring E, 4ds, p, 9ds.
Repeat from * till there are 8 flowers altogether, joining ring E of the final flower to ring A of the first. After working the final chain, cut and tie the ends to the beginning of the work.

The hand

Using shuttle thread only, ring of 3ds, join to picot of any chain on cuff, 3ds. Space of 1cm. *Ring of 3ds, join to next chain, 3ds. Space 1cm. Repeat from * all round cuff. Ring of 3ds, join to next space, 3ds.
Continue in rounds always leaving a space of 1cm between rings unless otherwise instructed. Mark the increases with a safety-pin.
Work 54 rings (counting from the beginning of the net), then increase. Continue with 48 rings, increase, 2 rings, increase, 70 rings, increase, 4 rings increase, 96 rings.
Miss 5 spaces for thumb opening and leave a space of 2cm on the shuttle thread before working the next ring. Continue in net for 105 more rings, working 2 rings into the 2cm space. After the final ring, reverse work for edging. Using ball and shuttle threads:
*Chain: 4ds, p, (2ds, p) twice, 4ds. Reverse work.
Using shuttle thread only:
Ring: 3ds, join to next space of previous round, 3ds. Reverse work. Repeat from * all round edge. Cut and tie ends to chain at beginning.

The thumb

Using shuttle thread only: (ring of 3ds, join to centre of double space at back of thumb opening, 3ds, space of 1cm) twice. Ring of 3ds, join to half space at side of opening, 3ds. Space of 1cm.
(Rings of 3ds, join to next space of front thumb, 3ds, space of 1cm) 5 times
Ring of 3ds, join to half space at side of openings, 3ds. Space of 1cm. Ring of 3ds, join to next space of round, 3ds. Space of 1cm.
Continue in rounds, leaving the usual space of 1cm between rings (unless decreasing). Work 7 rings, decrease, 7 rings, decrease 7 rings, then work edging as given for hand.
Work a second mitten.

To finish

Press cuffs and edgings under a damp cloth.

Thread shirring elastic through the centres of 6 rings at the front of the wrist only. Tie the ends of the elastic inside the glove adjusting the tension as required.

To measure the mesh

Cut a small rectangle of card the width equal to the space required between rings. Grip this between the forefinger and thread to gauge the space. Keep the card in position while the half ring is worked. Remove it after working the space and repeat for the rest of the net.

To tie a chain using the shuttle thread join

Insert the hook into the picot where the chain is to be joined, catch the shuttle thread and pull it out into a loop. Pass the shuttle through this loop, position the resultant knot against the last double stitch of the chain and tighten the knot.
Continue in pattern as required.

Chapter 4

Knitted Lace

The effects of knitted lace can be as delicate and pretty as any form of traditional lace. Although it is commonly thought to be knitted on extremely fine needles, some of the loveliest and simplest patterns use average size needles.

The laciness is created by deliberately made holes, formed largely by decorative increasing and decreasing stitches worked into a pattern repeat. Its overall beauty ultimately depends on how evenly these stitches are worked.

The projects given in the following pages begin with a pretty edging for placemats — a traditional pattern, with the delightful name of Oyster shell, which would make an ideal beginner's project — and progress through more elaborate designs for tablecloths, curtains and cushions, to a spectacular lace collar suitable for the more experienced knitter.

Lacy tablemats

Crisp white linen edged with delicate knitted lace lends a gracious note to the most elegant dinner parties. The place settings, each comprising a plate mat and coaster, are matched by a large oval centrepiece.

Materials

Lacy edgings should be worked in a yarn which complements the main garment or object. Fine cotton, linen or even silk yarns, or synthetics with the properties of these fibres are especially suitable for edgings on household linens and on summer garments. Textured yarns are not usually appropriate for lacy patterns in general as the stitch detail tends to be obscured by the yarn.

Size

Plate mat 29cm diameter including edging
Coaster 24cm diameter including edging
Centrepiece 53 by 41cm including edging

Tension

25 stitches and 30 rows to 5cm over garter stitch on 2¾mm needles

Abbreviations

The following abbreviations are used in knitting patterns:

alt	alternately
beg	begin(ning)
cont	continu(e)(ing)
dec	decrease
foll	following
inc	increase
K	knit
K2 tog	knit two together
k-wise	knitwise
LH	left hand
patt	pattern
psso	pass slipped stitch over
p	purl
p-wise	purlwise
rem	remaining
rep	repeat
RH	right hand
RS	right side
sl	slip
st	stitches
tbl	through back of loop
WS	wrong side
yfwd	yarn forward
yon	yarn over needle

You will need

For six place settings and one centrepiece:
Five 20g balls of Coats Chain Mercer Crochet No. 60 cotton
1 pair 2¾mm knitting needles
0.70m of 90cm-wide medium-weight linen
4 skeins coton à broder
No. 7 crewel needle
Cartridge paper

Making the templates

Using the cartridge paper cut out two templates — a circle 14cm in diameter for the coaster and another 19cm in diameter for the plate mat. For the centrepiece trace and cut out the overprinted shape given below. This represents a quarter of the template for the centrepiece. To make a full template take a sheet of cartridge paper 45cm by 35cm and fold it in half twice.

Place the right angle of the quarter template on the right angle of the folds, trace round it and cut it out.

Coaster edging

Using 2¾mm needles cast on 25 sts. Knit one row.
Work in pattern as follows:
1st row Sl 1, K2, P6, K3, yrn twice, K to end. 27 sts.
2nd row Yrn, K2 tog, K11, P1, K to end.
3rd row Sl 1, K2, P6, K to end.
4th row Yrn, K2 tog, K to end.
5th row Sl 1, K2, P6, K3, yrn twice, K2 tog, yrn twice, K2 tog, K to end. 29 sts.
6th row Yrn, K2 tog, K10, P1, K2, P1, K to end.
7th row Sl 1, K2, P6, K to end.
8th row Yrn, K2 tog, K8, turn, K to end.
9th row Yrn, K2 tog, K7, K2 tog, K9, sl the 4th, 5th and 6th sts on LH needle over 1st, 2nd and 3rd sts, yfwd, K3, yfwd, K3. 27 sts.
10th row Sl 1, K2, P6, K3, (yrn twice, K2 tog) 3 times, K to end. 30 sts.
11th row Yrn, K2 tog, K9, P1, K2, P1, K2, P1, K to end.
12th row Sl 1, K2, P6, K to end.
13th row Yrn, K2 tog, K7, turn, K to end.
14th row Yrn, K2 tog, K6, K2 tog, K to end. 29 sts.
15th row Sl 1, K2, P6, K3, (yrn twice, K2 tog) 4 times, K to end. 33 sts.
16th row Yrn, K2 tog, K9, (P1, K2) 3 times, P1, K to end.
17th row Sl 1, K2, P6, K15, sl all but last st over first st on LH needle, K2 tog. 25 sts.
18th row Yrn, K2 tog, K14, sl the 4th, 5th and 6th sts on LH needle over 1st, 2nd and 3rd sts, yrn, K3, yrn, K1, pick up loop between last st knitted and next st and K into back of it, K2. 25 sts.
Repeat 1st-18th rows approximately 15 times more or until edging when stretched fits around the circumference of the coaster template.
Cast off loosely leaving enough yarn to join the row edges.

Plate mat edging

Work as given for the coaster edging, repeating the pattern approximately 21 times or until the edging when stretched fits the circumference of the plate mat template.
Complete as given for the coaster.

Centrepiece edging

Work as given for the coaster edging, repeating the pattern approximately 35 times or until the edging when stretched fits the circumference of the centrepiece template.
Complete as given for the coaster.

To make up

Pin out the edgings to shape stretching them slightly to the correct measurements and press under a damp cloth. Join the row ends of each edging to make a circle by picking up and sewing through one thread at a time on each edge joining the pattern. Using a fairly hot iron, press the linen under a damp cloth to remove any creases.
To finish the mats, see Attaching the edging.

Attaching the edging

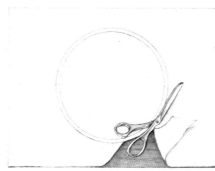

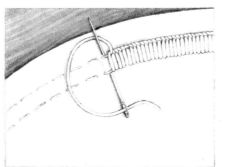

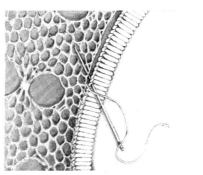

1 Place the templates on the wrong side of the linen and, using a soft pencil, draw round the required number of circles leaving at least 2cm between each one. Cut out the circles adding 1cm of fabric allowance all round.

2 Using coton à broder work a row of running stitches on the pencil line and another just inside it. On the right side work buttonhole stitch over the stitching lines.

3 Cut away the excess fabric allowance close to the line of buttonhole stitch. Slipstitch the lace edgings to the loops of the buttonhole stitch.

Centrepiece trace pattern

Viennese lace cloth

This delicate lace cloth is exquisite enough for a cherished heirloom but also perfectly practical for everyday use as an elegant coffee table or tray cloth.

Materials

The traditional yarn for Viennese lace knitting is fine to medium crochet cotton like that used for the coffee table cloth, or occasionally, linen thread of a similar thickness. The most popular colours are white and écru. As is the case with most types of lace knitting, the finished work requires careful stretching if the full beauty of the stitches is to be displayed. Items like tablecloths, doilies and mats also benefit from a light starching which helps them retain their shape in use. Wash, rinse and starch the completed lace and leave it wet for stretching. Alternatively, use a spray starch on the lace after it has been pinned out as shown opposite.

Tension

32 stitches and 36 rows to 10cm over pattern on 2¾mm needles

Abbreviations

See page 82

You will need

For a tablecloth, 50cm in diameter

Two 20g balls of Coats Chain Mercer No. 20 crochet cotton
Set of four 2¾mm knitting needles pointed at both ends
Cable needle
1.25mm crochet hook

To make

Using three of the set of four needles, cast on 8 sts. Arrange 3 sts on the first and second needles and 2 sts on the third needle. Join into a ring.
Work in rounds as follows:
1st round K to end.
2nd round (K1, P1) into each st. 16 sts.
3rd round *K2, yfwd, rep from * to end. 24 sts.
4th and following alternate rounds K to end.
5th round *K2, yfwd, K1, yfwd, rep from * to end. 40 sts.
7th round *K2, yfwd, (K1, yfwd) 3 times, rep from * to end. 72 sts.
9th round *K2, sl 1, K1, psso, yfwd, (K1, yfwd) 3 times, K2 tog, rep from * to end. 88 sts.

11th round *K2, sl 1, K1, psso, (K1, yfwd) 4 times, K1, K2 tog, rep from * to end. 104 sts.
13th round *Yfwd, K2, yfwd, sl 1, K1, psso, K3, yfwd, K1, yfwd, K3, K2 tog, rep from * to end. 120 sts.
15th round *Yfwd, K1, yfwd, K2, yfwd, K1, yfwd, K4, sl 1, K1, psso, K5, rep from * to end. 144 sts.
17th round *Yfwd, K2 tog, yrn twice, K1 tbl, K2, K1 tbl, yrn twice, sl 1, K1, psso, yfwd, K4, sl 1, K1, psso, K4, rep from * to end. 168 sts.
18th round K to end, working P1, K1 into yrn twice of previous round.
19th round *Yfwd, K3, K2 tog, yfwd, K2, yfwd, sl 1, K1, psso, K3, yfwd, K4, sl 1, K1, psso, K3, rep from * to end. 176 sts.
20th round K to end.
21st round *Yfwd, (K2, K2 tog, yrn twice, sl 1, K1, psso), twice, K2, yfwd, K4, sl 1, K1, psso, K2, rep from * to end. 184 sts.
22nd and following alternate rounds As 18th round.
23rd round *Yfwd, K1, K2 tog, yrn twice, sl 1, K1, psso, K2 tog, yfwd, K2, yfwd, sl 1, K1, psso, K2 tog, yrn twice, sl 1, K1, psso, K1, yfwd, K4, sl 1, K1, psso, K1, rep from * to end. 192 sts.
25th round *K2 tog, yrn twice, sl 1, K1, psso, sl 1, K2 tog, psso, yfwd, K1, yfwd, K2, K2 tog, yrn twice, sl 1, K1, psso, K2 tog, yrn twice, sl 1, K1, psso, yfwd, K4, sl 1, K1, psso, rep from * to end.
27th round *Yfwd, sl 1, K1, psso, K1, K2 tog, (yfwd, K1) 3 times, yfwd, K2, yfwd, sl 1, K1, psso, K2 tog, yrn twice, sl 1, K1, psso, K3, yfwd, sl 1, K1, psso, K3, rep from * to end. 216 sts.
29th round *K2 tog, yrn twice, (sl 1, K1, psso) twice, (yfwd, K1) 3 times, yfwd, K2 tog, K2, K2 tog, yrn twice, sl 1, K1, psso, K2 tog, yrn twice, sl 1, K1, psso, K2, yfwd, sl 1, K1, psso, K2, rep from * to end. 232 sts.
31st round *Yfwd, sl 1, K1, psso, K2 tog, yfwd, sl 1, K1, psso, (K1, yfwd) 4 times, K1, K2 tog, K2, yfwd, sl 1, K1, psso, K2 tog, yrn twice, sl 1, K1, psso, K2 tog, yrn twice, sl 1, K1, psso, K1, yfwd, sl 1, K1, psso, K1, rep from * to end. 248 sts.

33rd round *K2 tog, yrn twice, (sl 1, K1, psso) twice, K3, yfwd, K1, yfwd, K3, K2 tog, yfwd, K2, (K2 tog, yrn twice, sl 1, K1, psso) twice, K2 tog, yrn twice, (K2 tog) twice, rep from * to end.
35th round *Yfwd, sl 1, K1, psso, K2 tog, yfwd, K5, K2 tog, K4, yfwd, K1, yfwd, K2, yfwd, sl 1, K1, psso, (K2 tog, yrn twice, sl 1, K1, psso) twice, yfwd, K3 tog, yrn, rep from * to end. 256 sts.
37th round *K2 tog, yrn twice, sl 1, K1, psso, K4, K2 tog, K4, yfwd, K2 tog, yrn twice, K1 tbl, K2, (K2 tog, yrn twice, sl 1, K1, psso) twice, K2 tog, yfwd, (P1, K1) into next st, yfwd, K2, rep from * to end. 280 sts.
39th round *Yfwd, sl 1, K1, psso, K2 tog, yfwd, K3, K2 tog, K4, yfwd, K3, K2 tog, yfwd, K2, yfwd, sl 1, K1, psso, K2 tog, yrn twice, sl 1, K1, psso, K3 tog, yfwd, K4, yfwd, K2 tog, yrn, rep from * to end.
41st round *K2 tog, yrn twice, sl 1, K1, psso, K2, K2 tog, K4, yfwd, K2, K2 tog, yrn twice, sl 1, K1, psso, K2, K2 tog, yrn twice, sl 1, K1, psso, K3 tog, yfwd, K6, yfwd, K2, rep from * to end.
43rd round *Yfwd, sl 1, K1, psso, K2 tog, yfwd, K1, K2 tog, K4, yfwd, K1, K2 tog, yrn twice, sl 1, K1, psso, K2 tog, yfwd, K2, yfwd, sl 1, K1, psso, K3 tog, yfwd K8, yfwd, K2 tog, yrn, rep from * to end.
45th round *K2 tog, yrn twice, sl 1, K1, psso, K2 tog, K4, yfwd, (K2 tog, yrn twice, sl 1, K1, psso) twice, yfwd, K2, K3 tog, K10, yfwd, sl 1, K1, psso, rep from * to end. 272 sts.
47th round *Yfwd, sl 1, K1, psso, K2 tog, (yfwd, K3, K2 tog) twice, yrn twice, sl 1, K1, psso, K3, yfwd, K1, K2 tog, K1 tbl, K8, K1 tbl, yfwd, K2 tog, yrn, rep from * to end. 280 sts.
49th round *K2 tog, yrn twice, sl 1, K1, psso, K2, K2 tog, yfwd, K2, K2 tog, yrn twice, sl 1, K1, psso, K2 tog, yrn twice, sl 1, K1, psso, K2, yfwd, K2, sl 1, K1, psso, K6, K2 tog, yfwd, K3, rep from * to end.
51st round *Yfwd, sl 1, K1, psso, K2 tog, (yfwd, K1, K2 tog) twice, (yrn twice, sl 1, K1, psso, K2 tog) twice, yrn twice, sl 1, K1, psso, K1, yfwd, K2, sl 1, K1, psso, K4, K2 tog,

yfwd, K2, K2 tog, yrn, rep from * to end.

53rd round *K2 tog, yrn twice, sl 1, K1, psso, (K2 tog) twice, (yrn twice, sl 1, K1, psso, K2 tog) 3 times, yrn twice, sl 1, K1, psso, K2, sl 1, K1, psso, K2, K2 tog, yfwd, K1, K2 tog, yrn twice, sl 1, K1, psso, rep from * to end. 264 sts.

55th round *Yfwd, sl 1, K1, psso, K3 tog, (yrn twice, sl 1, K1, psso, K2 tog) 4 times, yfwd, K2, sl 1, K1, psso, (K2 tog) twice, yrn twice, sl 1,

K1, psso, K2 tog, yrn, rep from * to end. 240 sts.

56th round K20, *sl next 4 sts on to cable needle, wind yarn round these 4 sts 12 times, K 4 sts from cable needle, K26, rep from * ending last rep K6.

56th round *K2 tog, (yrn twice, sl 1, K1, psso, K2 tog) 4 times, yrn twice, sl 1, K1, psso, K4 tog, yrn twice, sl 1, K1, psso, K2 tog, yrn twice, sl 1, K1, psso, rep from * to end. 224 sts.

58th and following alternate rounds

As 18th round.

59th round Yfwd, *sl 1, K1, psso, K2 tog, yrn twice, rep from * to last 4 sts, sl 1, K1, psso, K2 tog, yfwd.

61st round *K2 tog, yrn twice, sl 1, K1, psso, rep from * to end.

62nd round As 58th round.

63rd-76 rounds Rep 59th-62nd rounds 3 times more, then 59th-60th rounds once more.

77th round *(K1, P1) into next st, K13, yrn 3 times, rep from * to end. 288 sts.

Yarn forward (yfwd)

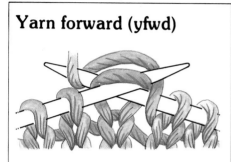

This method is used to make a stitch between two knit stitches. After the first knit stitch bring the yarn forward between the needles and knit the next stitch as usual.

78th round K to end, working P1, K1, P1 into yrn 3 times of previous round.

79th round *Sl 1, K1, psso, K11, K2 tog, (yfwd, K1) 3 times, yfwd, rep from * to end. 320 sts.

80th and following alternate rounds K.

81st round *Sl 1, K1, psso, K9, (K2 tog, yfwd) twice, K3, yfwd, sl 1, K1, psso, yfwd, rep from * to end.

83rd round *Sl 1, K1, psso, K7, (K2 tog, yfwd) 3 times, K1, (yfwd, sl 1, K1, psso) twice, yfwd, rep from * to end.

85th round *Sl 1, K1, psso, K5, (K2 tog, yfwd) 3 times, K3, (yfwd, sl 1, K1, psso) twice, yfwd, rep from * to end.

87th round *Sl 1, K1, psso, K3, (K2 tog, yfwd) 4 times, K1, (yfwd, sl 1, K1, psso) 3 times, yfwd, rep from * to end.

89th round *Sl 1, K1, psso, K1, (K2 tog, yfwd) 4 times, K3, (yfwd, sl 1, K1, psso) 3 times, yfwd, rep from * to end.

91st round *K3 tog, (yfwd, K2 tog) 4 times, yfwd, K1, (yfwd, sl 1, K1, psso) 4 times, yfwd, rep from * to end.

92nd round K.

K 2 sts from first needle on to end of third needle.

Working the scalloped edging

Using the crochet hook cast off as follows:

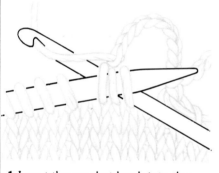

1 Insert the crochet hook into the back of the next three stitches on the left-hand needle.

2 Work one double crochet through these three stitches to bring them together, keeping the stitches on the needle until the double crochet is completed. Ease the stitches towards the point.

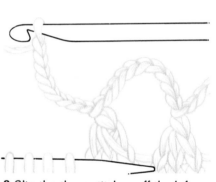

3 Slip the three stitches off the left-hand needle. Work ten chain stitches. Repeat from the beginning.

Insert hook into back of next 5 sts on LH needle work 1dc and slip sts off needle, 10ch, (inserting hook into back of next 3 sts on LH needle work 1dc and slip sts off needle, 10ch) 3 times, repeat from the beginning. Continue in this way around the edge of the cloth until all the stitches have been cast off. Join the last chain to the first double crochet with a slip stitch. Fasten off.

To make up

Dampen the work (or it can be washed in warm water using soap flakes, thoroughly rinsed and starched).

Draw a circle 50cm in diameter on a sheet of white paper. Place this over a thick pad (for example, a folded towel or blanket). While the cloth is still damp pin it out to the measurement of the

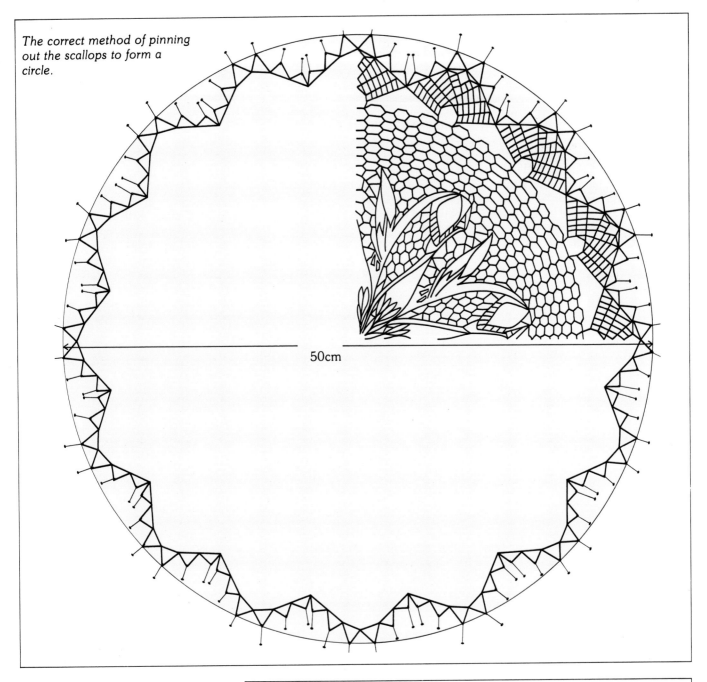

The correct method of pinning out the scallops to form a circle.

50cm

circle. Pin the centre of the cloth to the centre of the circle, then pin the centre of the two crochet-cast-off scallops on the outer points of the lace to the circumference of the circle, drawing each one out into a point. Pin the remaining scallops out similarly using the diagram given for guidance. The lace should be stretched to the fullest possible extent so if the circle is too small draw another one slightly larger.

If the cloth has not already been starched during washing, spray it with spray starch. This helps to keep a longer-lasting freshness. Leave it until it is completely dry. Pin out the cloth in this way after every washing. Extra pressing is not usually necessary.

Slip one, knit one, pass slipped stitch over (sl 1, K1, psso)

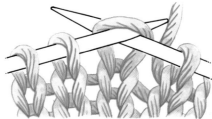

1 Insert the right-hand needle into the next stitch on the left-hand needle as if to knit it. Slip the stitch off the needle on to the right-hand needle.

2 Knit the next stitch on the left-hand needle as usual. With the point of the left-hand needle, lift up the slipped stitch, pass it over the stitch just knitted and off the needle.

Filet lace curtain

Give a sunny window a fresh summery look with a crisp white lacy curtain, shaped on the inner edges to suggest a draped look.

Materials

Filet lace knitting is best worked in fine smooth cotton yarns. Anything fluffy or texured will tend to obscure the mesh pattern completely. After working the pattern the fabric benefits from being slightly stretched and starched, making the motifs sharp-edged and clearly defined against the mesh background. The technique is more suited to geometric designs than representational motifs. The filet curtain has been worked in a fine mercerized cotton yarn.

Tension

34 stitches and 68 rows to 10cm over garter stitch on 2¼mm needles.

Abbreviations

See page 82

You will need

For a curtain, 84cm long by 72cm wide

Four 50g balls of Phildar Relais No. 5
1 pair 2¼mm knitting needles

Right side panel

Using 2¼mm needles, cast on 48sts.
1st-7th rows K.
8th row K5, *make a space thus, yrn twice, sl 2 K-wise, pass 2nd st on RH needle over 1st st and off needle, sl 1 K-wise, pass 2nd st on RH needle over 1st st and off needle, insert LH needle back into 1st st on RH needle and K it, — called make 1 space — K3, make 4 spaces, K3, Make 6 spaces, ** K4.
9th and every following alternate row K to end, purling 2nd yrn sts of previous row.
10th, 12th and 14th rows As 8th row.
16th and 18th rows K5, *make 1 space, K3, make 4 spaces, K3, make 2 spaces, K6, make 2 spaces, ** K4.
20th, 22nd, 24th and 26th rows As 16th row.
28th, 30th, 32nd and 34th rows As 8th row.
36th and 38th rows K5, *make 1 space, K3, make 4 spaces, K21, ** K4.

40th and 42nd rows As 36th row.
44th and 46th rows K5, *make 1 space, K3, make 9 spaces, K3, make 1 space, ** K4.
48th, 50th, 52nd and 54th rows As 44th row.
56th and 58th rows K5, *make 1 space, K21, make 3 spaces, K3, make 1 space, ** K4.
59th row Cast on 15 sts, K to end, purling the 2nd yrn sts of previous row.
60th and 62nd rows K5, *make 1 space, K21, make 3 spaces, K21, ** K4.
64th and 66th rows K5, *make 1 space, K3, make 5 spaces, K3, make 3 spaces, K21, ** K4.
68th and 70th rows K5, *make 1 space, K3, make 5 spaces, K3, make 3 spaces, K3, make 6 spaces, ** K4.
72nd and 74th rows K5, *make 1 space, K9, (make 3 spaces, K3) twice, make 6 spaces, ** K4.
76th and 78 rows K5, *make 1 space, K9, (make 3 spaces, K3) twice, make 2 spaces, K6, make 2 spaces, ** K4.
80th, 82nd, 84th and 86th rows K5, * (make 1 space, K3) twice, (make 3 spaces, K3) twice, make 2 spaces, K6, make 2 spaces, ** K4.
88th, 90th, 92nd and 94th rows K5, * (make 1 space, K3) twice, (make 3 spaces, K3) twice, make 6 spaces, ** K4.
96th, 98th, 100th and 102nd rows K5, * (make 1 space, K3) twice, make 3 spaces, K3, make 3 spaces, K21, ** K4.
104th, 106th, 108th and 110th rows K5, * (make 1 space, K3) twice, make 3 spaces, K3, make 8 spaces, K3, make 1 space, ** K4.
112th, 114th, 116th and 118th rows K5 * (make 1 space, K3) twice, make 3 spaces, K18, make 3 spaces, K3, make 1 space, ** K4.
119th row Cast on 15 sts, K to end, purling 2nd yrn sts of previous row.
120th and 122nd rows K5, *(make 1 space, K3) twice, make 8 spaces, K3, make 3 spaces, K3, make 1 space, K15, ** K4.
124th and 126th rows K5, *(make 1 space, K3) twice, make 8 spaces,

K3, make 3 spaces, K21, ** K4.
128th, 130th, 132nd and 134th rows K5, *make 1 space, K3, make 1 space, K18, make 3 spaces, K3, make 3 spaces, K3, make 6 spaces, ** K4.
136th, 138th, 140th and 142nd rows K5, *make 1 space, K3, make 6 spaces, (K3, make 3 spaces) twice, K3, make 2 spaces, K6, make 2 spaces, ** K4.
144th and 146th rows K5, *make 1 space, K12, (make 3 spaces, K3) 3 times, make 2 spaces, K6, make 2 spaces, ** K4.
148th and 150th rows K5, *make 1 space, K12, (make 3 spaces, K3) 3 times, make 6 spaces, ** K4.
152nd and 154th rows K5, *make 1 space, K3, make 2 spaces, (K3, make 3 spaces) 3 times, K3, make 6 spaces, ** K4.
156th, 158th, 160th and 162nd rows K5, *make 1 space, K3, make 2 spaces, (K3, make 3 spaces) 3 times, K21, ** K4.
164th and 166th rows K5, *make 1 space, K3, make 2 spaces, (K3, make 3 spaces) twice, K3, make 9 spaces, K3, ** K4.
168th and 170th rows K5, *make 1 space, K66, ** K4.
172nd and 174th rows K5, *make 1 space, K6, (make 1 space, K3) 10 times, ** K4.
176th and 178th rows K5, *make 1 space, (K3, make 1 space) 10 times, K6, ** K4.
180th and 182nd rows As 172nd.
184th and 186th rows As 168th row.
188th and 190th rows K5, *(make 1 space, K3) twice, make 16 spaces, K3, make 1 space, K3, ** K4.
192nd and 194th rows K5, *(make 1 space, K3) twice, make 7 spaces, K6, make 7 spaces, K3, make 1 space, K3, ** K4.
196th, 198th, 200th and 202nd rows K5, *(make 1 space, K3) twice, make 6 spaces, K12, make 6 spaces, K3, make 1 space, K3, ** K4.
204th and 206th rows K5, *(make 1 space, K3) twice, make 5 spaces, K6, make 2 spaces, K6, make 5 spaces, K3, make 1 space, K3, ** K4.

208th and **210th rows** K5, *(make 1 space, K3) twice, make 4 spaces, K9, make 2 spaces, K9, make 4 spaces, K3, make 1 space, K3, ** K4.

212th and **214th rows** K5, *(make 1 space, K3) twice, (make 4 spaces, K6) twice, make 4 spaces, K3, make 1 space, K3, ** K4.

216th and **218th rows** K5, *(make 1 space, K3) twice, make 3 spaces, K9, make 4 spaces, K9, make 3 spaces,

K3, make 1 space, K3, **K4.

220th and **222nd rows** K5, *(make 1 space, K3) twice, make 2 spaces, K9, make 6 spaces, K9, make 2 spaces, K3, make 1 space, K3, ** K4.

224th and **226th rows** As 220th row.

228th and **230th rows** As 216th row.

232nd and **234th rows** As 212th

row.

236th and **238th rows** As 208th row.

240th and **242nd rows** As 204th row.

244th, 246th, 248th and **250th rows** As 196th row.

252nd and **254th rows** As 192nd row.

256th and **258th rows** As 188th row.

260th and 262nd rows As 168th row.

264th and 266th rows As 172nd row.

268th and 270th rows As 176th row.

272nd and 274th rows As 172nd row.

276th and 278th rows As 168th row.

280th-287th rows K.
Cast off.

Left side panel

Using 2¼mm needles, cast on 48 sts.

1st-7th rows K.

8th row K4, work from ** to * as given for 8th row of right side panel, K5.

9th and every following alternate row K to end, purling the 2nd yrn sts of previous row.

10th, 12th and 14th rows As 8th row.

16th and 18th rows K4, work from ** to * as given for 16th row of right side panel, K5.

Continue in this way, reversing the pattern given for the right side panel, casting on 15 sts at the beginning of the 60th and 120th rows instead of the 59th and 119th rows.

Work with an even tension throughout.

Centre panel

Using 2¼mm needles, cast on 48 sts.

1st-7th rows K.

***8th and 10th rows** K5, (make 1 space, K3) 6 times, make 1 space, K4.

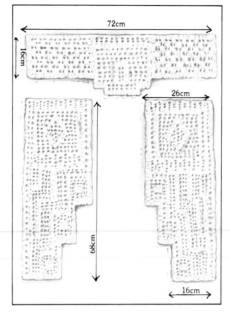

9th and every following alternate row K to end, purling the 2nd yrn sts of previous row.

12th and 14th rows K5, (K3, make 1 space) 6 times, K7.

15th row As 9th row.

Repeat 8th-15th rows inclusive 11 times more, then 8th-10th rows inclusive once more. ***

Commence shaped section

1st rows Cast on 12 sts, K to end.

2nd-8th rows K.

9th, 11th, 13th and 15th rows K5, make 8 spaces, (K3, made 1 space) 4 times, make 1 space, K4.

10th and every following alternate row K to end, purling 2nd yrn sts of previous row.

17th row Cast on 12 sts, K17, make 8 spaces, (K3, make 1 space) 4 times, make 1 space, K4.

19th, 21st and 23rd rows K17, make 8 spaces, (K3, make 1 space) 4 times, make 1 space, K4.

25th, 27th, 29th and 31st rows K5, make 12 spaces, (K3, make 1 space) 4 times, make 1 space, K4.

33rd, 35th, 37th and 39th rows K5, make 2 spaces, K24, make 2 spaces, (K3, make 1 space) 4 times, make 1 space, K4.

41st and 43rd rows K5, make 2 spaces, K6, make 4 spaces, K6, make 2 spaces, (K3, make 1 space) 4 times, make 1 space, K4.

45th, 47th, 49th and 51st rows As 33rd row.

53rd, 55th, 57th and 59th rows As 25th row.

61st, 63rd, 65th and 67th rows As 19th row.

69th row Cast off 12 sts, K5 including st used in casting off, make 8 spaces, (K3, make 1 space) 4 times, make 1 space, K4.

71st, 73rd and 75th rows As 9th row.

76th row As 10th row.

77th-83rd rows K.

Casting off 12 sts at beg of next row work from *** to ***. K 7 rows.
Cast off.

To make up

Pin out the pieces to the exact size and shape required and press. Sew the side panels to the centre panel as follows:

Joining the seams

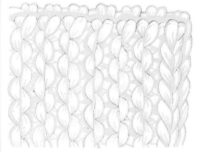

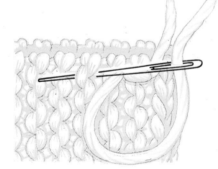

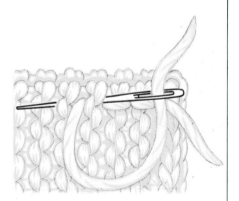

1 The sections of the filet curtain are joined with a back-stitch seam. Place the edges to be joined with right sides together, carefully matching the pieces

2 Thread a blunt-ended wool needle with matching yarn and begin at the right-hand end of the seam securing the end of the yarn with a double stitch. Make a stitch by pushing the needle through both layers and bringing it back again to the front of the seam.

3 Insert the needle back into the fabric as shown and bring it to the front again. Continue in this way to the end of the seam.
Finally, pin the curtain to a towel, and press. Use a spray starch as directed on the can to hold the shape.

Working the mesh

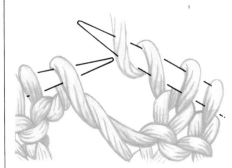

1 Each space in the mesh occupies three stitches worked as follows. Bring the yarn forward and then take it back over the needle, then forward again.

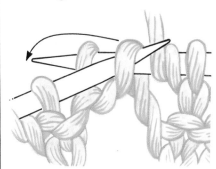

2 Slip the next stitch knitwise. Slip the following stitch knitwise. Pass the first slipped stitch over the second slipped stitch and off the needle.

3 Slip the next stitch knitwise. Pass the second slipped stitch over the third slipped stitch and off the needle.

4 Insert the left-hand needle back into the third slipped stitch and knit it.

5 On the following row, knit every stitch but purl the second loop taken over the needle in step 1.

Working the blocks

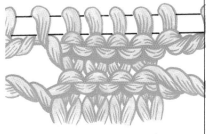

Each block is worked over three stitches which combine, when spaces and blocks are alternated, with the last stitch of the previous space to make a block of four stitches in width. The block is squared by knitting on these stitches for four rows so that each block must have two spaces in depth on either side.

Using filet charts

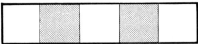

Filet knitting is often worked from special charts. The open squares represent the spaces and the solid squares the blocks. Each row of squares takes four knitting rows to complete. The first row of the chart represents the 1st-4th rows, the second row represents the 5th-8th rows and so on.

Calculating the cast-on stitches

Allow three stitches for every block and space on the bottom row of the chart. In addition, unless otherwise indicated, allow for five edge stitches not represented on the chart. Work three edge stitches in garter stitch at the right-hand side and two edge stitches on the left-hand side. Here the number of cast-on stitches would be twenty.

Converting the chart

Instructions for the bottom row of the chart given would read thus. Cast on 20 stitches.

1st and 3rd rows K3, (yrn twice, sl 2 K-wise, pass 2nd st on RH needle over 1st st and off needle, sl 1 K-wise, pass 2nd st on RH needle over 1st st and off needle, insert LH needle back into 1st st on RH needle and K it — called make one space — K3) twice, make one space, K2.

2nd and 4th rows K4, (P1, K5) twice, P1, K3.

The first row of the chart is now completed.

The rest of the chart can be worked directly from the chart itself, working blocks and spaces as indicated plus the edge stitches.

Chevron pillow

Use white or a delicate pastel coloured cotton to make this pretty cushion cover. This particular chevron pattern, called Horseshoe or Willow pattern is worked on the front only for a lacy effect. Work a separate edging and join on neatly afterwards.

Materials
Choose your yarn carefully when making chevrons. It is best to use a fine Shetland yarn or cotton. Avoid using chunky and hairy type yarns so as not to obscure the stitch detail. To be really sure of the finished effect, work a sample in your chosen yarn before embarking on the cushion cover. (See working the Horseshoe pattern.)

Tension
20 stitches and 28 rows to 10cms over pattern on 4mm needles.

Abbreviations
See page 82

You will need
To fit a cushion, 30cm by 30cm

Four 25g Twilleys Lyscordet cotton
One pair of 4mm needles
Small fastenings

Front
Using 4mm needles cast on 71 sts.
1st and every alternate row (WS) P to end.
2nd row * K5, yon, ssk, K3, rep from * to last st, K1.
4th row * K3, K2 tog, yon, K1, yon, ssk, K1, rep from * to last st, K1.
6th row * K2, K2 tog, yon, K3, yon ssk, K1, rep from * to last st, K1.
8th row * K1, K2 tog, yon, K5, yon, ssk, rep from * to last st, K1.
10th row K2 tog, yon, K7, * yon, sl 1 K2 tog, psso, yon, K7, rep from * to last 2 sts, yon, ssk.
These 10 rows form the pattern,

repeat rows 1-10 inclusive 10 more times.
Cast off loosely.

Back
Using 4mm needles, cast on 71 sts. Starting with a K row work 108 rows in stocking stitch.
Cast off loosely.

Lace edge
Using 4mm needles cast on 13 sts.
1st and every alternate row (WS) K2, P to last 2 sts, K2.
2nd row Sl 1, K3, yon, K5, yon, K2 tog, yon, K2.
4th row Sl 1, K4, sl 1, K2, tog, psso, K2 (yon, K2 tog) twice, K1.
6th row Sl 1, K3, sl 1, K1, psso, K2 (yon, K2 tog) twice, K1.

Working the Horseshoe pattern

1 Horseshoe pattern chevrons are worked over a multiple of 10 stitches plus one extra stitch. For the sample, cast on 31 stitches by the two needle knit stitch cast-on method.

2 The first row is a wrong side row. Purl all the stitches on this row. The second row is the first of the right side rows. Knit the first stitch. Then work the 10 stitch pattern repeat. Bring the yarn forward over the needle, and knit the next three stitches.

3 Slip the next stitch, knit the next two stitches together, and pass the slipped stitch over. Knit the next three stitches, bring the yarn forward over the needle, and knit the next stitch.

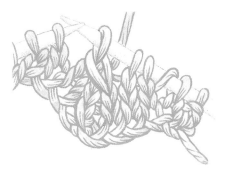

4 Return to the beginning of the 10 stitch pattern repeat, and repeat pattern until the end of the row is completed. Purl across all stitches on the next row fairly tightly.

5 Purl the first stitch of the fourth row, and then work the 10 stitch pattern repeat. Knit the first stitch, bring the yarn forward over the needle, and knit the next two stitches. Slip the next stitch, knit the next two stitches together, and pass the slipped stitch over.

6 Knit the next two stitches, bring the yarn forward over the needle, knit the next stitch, and purl the stitch after. Return to the beginning of the 10 stitch pattern repeat for the fourth row, and repeat this pattern to the end of the row.

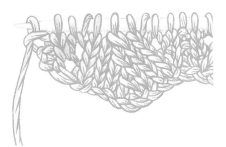

7 The fifth row is a wrong side row. Knit the first stitch. The 10 stitch pattern repeat for this row is purl nine stitches, knit one stitch. Repeat this pattern to the end of the row.

8 Purl the first stitch of the sixth row. Then work the 10 stitch pattern repeat. Knit the first two stitches, bring the yarn forward over the needle, and knit the next stitch. Slip the next stitch, knit the next two stitches together, and pass the slipped stitch over.

9 Knit the next stitch, bring the yarn forward over the needle, knit the next two stitches and purl the stitch after. Return to the beginning of the 10 stitch pattern repeat for the sixth row, and repeat this pattern until the end of the row is completed. The seventh row is worked as the fifth row, as shown in step 7.

  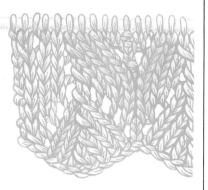

10 Purl the first stitch of the eighth row, and then work the 10 stitch pattern repeat. Knit the first three stitches, then bring the yarn forward over the needle. Slip the next stitch, knit the next two stitches together, and then pass the slipped stitch over.

11 Bring the yarn forward over the needle, knit the next three stitches, and purl the stitch after. Return to the beginning of the 10 stitch pattern repeat for the eighth row and repeat this pattern until the end of the row.

12 These eight rows form the pattern which should be repeated as required.

8th row Sl 1, K2, sl 1, K1, psso, K2, (yon, K2 tog) twice, K1.
10th row Sl 1, K1, sl 1, K1, psso, K2, (yon, K2 tog) twice, K1.
12th row K1, sl 1, K1, psso, K2, yon, K1, K2 tog, yon, K2.
14th row Sl 1, (K3, yon) twice, K2 tog, yon, K2.

These 14 rows form the pattern. Repeat rows 1-14 inclusive 41 times. Cast off loosely.

To make up
Press all the pieces with a warm iron and damp cloth. Sew the lace edging to the front, gathering the excess equally on all four sides. Sew the front to the back along three sides, leaving an opening to slip the cushion through. Secure the opening with tiny buttons or press studs.

Lace collar

Introduce a little old-fashioned elegance into your life with this exquisite lace collar. It transforms the plainest dress into something special.

Materials
To achieve the authentic look of lace use only the finest materials such as the No. 60 crochet cotton used in the collar. Fine silk thread has also been a favourite yarn for working knitted lace.

Whatever the yarn, lace knitting must always be stretched before pressing to reveal the full beauty of the stitch pattern. Generally it can be stretched to a third as much again as the cast-off width. Spray lightly with starch and press over a dry cloth.

Tension
40 stitches and 64 rows to 10cm over garter stitch on 2¼mm needles

Abbreviations
See page 82

You will need
For a collar, 18cm deep after stretching

One 20g ball of Coats Mercer
Crochet No. 60 cotton
1 pair 2¼mm knitting needles
1 small button

To make

Using 2¼mm needles, cast on 39 sts.
Next 2 rows P.
Commence the pattern.
1st row (RS) P20, K4, (yrn, P2 tog)
twice, K4, yfwd, sl 1, K1, psso, (yrn,
P2 tog) twice, K1.
2nd row K1, (yrn, p2 tog) 3 times,
K4, (yrn, P2 tog) twice, K4, P20.
3rd row P4, (yrn, K2 tog) 8 times,
K4, (yrn, P2 tog) twice, K3, K2 tog,
yfwd, K1, (yrn, P2 tog) twice, yrn,
(P1, K1) into last st.
4th row K1, yfwd, K2, (yrn, P2 tog)
twice, K2, yrn, P2 tog, K2, (yrn, P2
tog) twice, K4, P20.
5th row P4, (yon, K2, tog) 8 times,
K4, (yrn, P2 tog) twice, K1, K2 tog,
yfwd, K3, (yrn, P2 tog) twice, yrn,
K3, (P1, K1) into last st, turn, K1,
yfwd, K2, yrn, P2 tog, turn, yrn, P2
tog, yon, K3, (P1, K1) into last st.
6th row Cast off 5 sts, yrn, P2 tog,
K1, (yrn, P2 tog) twice, K4, (yrn, P2
tog) 3 times, K4, P20.
7th row P4, (yon, K2 tog) 8 times,
K4, (yrn, P2 tog) twice, yon, sl 1,
K1, psso, K4, (yrn, P2 tog) twice,
(P1, K1) into next st, yrn, P2 tog,
yrn, (P1, K1) into last st, make the
picot edge as follows, turn, K3, yrn,
P2 tog, turn, yrn, P2 tog, yon, K2,
yrn, (P1, K1) into last st, — called
make picot.
8th row Cast off 5 sts, yrn, P2 tog,
yon, K2, (yrn, P2 tog) twice, K3, P2
tog tbl, yrn, K1, (yrn, P2 tog) twice,
K4, P20.
9th row P4, (yon, K2 tog) 8 times,
K4, (yrn, P2 tog) twice, K2, yfwd, sl
1, K1, psso, K2, (yrn, P2 tog) twice,
K2, (P1, K1) into next st, yrn, P2
tog, yrn, (P1, K1) into last st, make
picot.
10th row Cast off 5sts, yrn, P2 tog,
yrn, K4, (yrn, P2 tog) twice, K1, P2
tog tbl, yon, K3, (yrn, P2 tog) twice,
K4, P20.
11th row P4, (yon, K2 tog) 8 times,
K4, (yrn, P2 tog) twice, K4, yfwd, sl
1, K1, psso, (yrn, P2 tog) twice, K4,
(P1, K1) into next st, yrn, P2 tog,
yrn, (P1, K1) into last st, make picot.
12th row Cast off 5 sts, yrn, P2 tog,
yrn, K6, (yrn, P2 tog) 3 times, K4,
(yrn, P2 tog) twice, K4, P20.
13th row P4, (yon, K2 tog) 8 times,
K4, (yrn, P2 tog) twice, K3, K2 tog,
yfwd, K1, (yrn, P2 tog) twice, K6,

(P1, K1) into next st, yrn, P2 tog,
yrn, (P1, K1) into last st, make picot.
14th row Cast off 5 sts, yrn, P2 tog,
yrn, K8, (yrn, P2 tog) twice, K2, yrn,
P2 tog, K2, (yrn, P2 tog) twice, K4,
P20.
15th row P4, (yon, K2 tog) 8 times,
K4, (yrn, P2 tog) twice, K1, K2 tog,
yfwd, K3, (yrn, P2 tog) twice, K8,
(P1, K1) into next st, yrn, P2 tog,
yrn, (P1, K1) into last st, make picot.
16th row Cast off 5sts, yrn, P2 tog,
yrn, P3 tog, K7, (yrn, P2 tog) twice,
K4, (yrn, P2 tog) 3 times, K4, P20.
17th row P4, (yrn, K2 tog) 8 times,
K4, (yrn, P2 tog) twice, yon, sl 1,
K1, psso, K4, (yrn, P2 tog) twice,
K6, K2 tog, K1, yrn, P2 tog, yrn,
(P1, K1) into last st, make picot.
18th row Cast off 5 sts, yrn, P2 tog,
yrn, P3 tog, K5, (yrn, P2 tog) twice,
K3, P2 tog tbl, yrn, K1, (yrn, P2 tog)
twice, K4, P20.
19th row P4, (yon, K2 tog) 8 times,
K4, (yrn, P2 tog) twice, K2, yfwd, sl
1, K1, psso, K2, (yrn, P2 tog) twice,
K4, K2 tog, K1, yrn, P2 tog, yrn,
(P1, K1) into last st, make picot.
20th row Cast off 5 sts, yrn, P2 tog,
yrn, P3 tog, K3, (yrn, P2 tog) twice,
K1, P2 tog tbl, yrn, K3, (yrn, P2 tog)
twice, K4, P20.
21st row P4, (yrn, K2 tog) 8 times,
K4, (yrn, P2 tog) twice, K4, yfwd, sl
1, K1, psso, (yrn, P2 tog) twice, K2,
K2 tog, K1, yrn, P2 tog, yrn, (P1,
K1) into last st, make picot.

22nd row Cast off 5, yrn, P2 tog,
yrn, P3 tog, K1, (yrn, P2 tog) 3
times, K4, (yrn, P2 tog) twice, K4,
P20.
23rd row P4, (yon, K2 tog) 8 times,
K4, (yrn, P2 tog) twice, K3, K2 tog,
yfwd, K1, (yrn, P2 tog) twice, K2
tog, K1, yrn, P2 tog, yrn, (P1, K1)
into last st, make picot.
24th row Cast off 5, yrn, P2 tog
twice, (yrn, P2 tog) twice, K2, yrn,
P2 tog, K2, (yrn, P2 tog) twice, K4,
P20.
25th row P4, (yon, K2 tog) 8 times,
K4, (yrn, P2 tog) twice, K1, K2 tog,
yfwd, K3, (yrn, P2 tog) twice, sl 1,
K2 tog, psso, K1.
26th row K2 tog, (yrn, P2 tog) twice,
K4, (yrn, P2 tog) 3 times, K4, P20.
27th row P4, (yon, K2 tog) 8 times,
K4, (yrn, P2 tog) twice, yon, sl 1,
K1, psso, K4, (yrn, P2 tog) twice,
K1.
28th row K1, (yrn, P2 tog) twice,
K3, P2 tog tbl, yon, K1, (yrn, P2 tog)
twice, K4, P20.
29th row P4, (yon, K2 tog) 8 times,
K4, (yrn, P2 tog) twice, K2, yfwd, sl
1, K1, psso, K2, (yrn, P2 tog) twice,
K1.
30th row K1, (yrn, P2 tog) twice,
K1, P2 tog tbl, yon, K3, (yrn, P2 tog)
twice, K4, P20.
31st row P4, (yrn, K2 tog) 8 times,
K4, (yrn, P2 tog) twice, K4, yfwd, sl
1, K1, psso, (yrn, P2 tog) twice, K1.
32nd row K1, (yrn, P2 tog) 3 times,

K4, (yrn, P2 tog) twice, K4, turn, K4, (yrn, P2 tog) twice, K3, K2 tog, yrn, K1, (yrn, P2 tog) twice, yrn, (P1, K1) into last st.

33rd row K1, yfwd, K2, (yrn, P2 tog) twice, K2, yrn, P2 tog, K2, (yrn, P2 tog) twice, K4, P1, turn, P1, K4, (yrn, P2 tog) twice, K1, K2 tog, yfwd, K3, (yrn, P2 tog) twice, yon, K3, (P1, K1) into last st, turn, K1, yfwd, K2, yrn, P2 tog, turn, yrn, P2 tog, yon, K3, (P1, K1) into last st.

34th row Cast off 5 sts, yrn, P2 tog, K1, (yrn, P2 tog) twice, K4, (yrn, P2 tog) 3 times, K4, P2, turn, P2, K4, (yrn, P2 tog) twice, yon, sl 1, K1, psso, K4, (yrn, P2 tog) twice, (P1, K1) into next st, yrn, P2 tog, yrn, (P1, K1) into last st, make picot.

35th row Cast off 5 sts, yrn, P2 tog, yon, K2, (yrn, P2 tog) twice, K3, P2 tog tbl, yon, K1, (yrn, P2 tog) twice, K4, P3, turn, P3, K4, (yrn, P2 tog) twice, K2, yfwd, sl 1, K1, psso, K2, (yrn, P2 tog) twice, K2, (P1, K1) into next st, yrn, P2 tog, yrn, (P1, K1) into last st, make picot.

36th row Cast off 5 sts, yrn, P2 tog, yon, K4, (yrn, P2 tog) twice, K1, P2 tog tbl, yon, K3, (yrn, P2 tog) twice, K4, P4, turn, P4, K4, (yrn, P2 tog) twice, K4, yfwd, sl 1, K1, psso, (yrn, P2 tog) twice, K4, (P1, K1) into next st, yrn, P2 tog, yrn, (P1, K1) into last st, make picot.

37th row Cast off 5 sts, yrn, P2 tog, yrn, K6, (yrn, P2 tog) 3 times, K4, (yrn, P2 tog) twice, K4, P5, turn, P5, K4, (yrn, P2 tog) twice, K3, K2 tog,

yfwd, K1, (yrn, P2 tog) twice, K6, (P1, K1) into next st, yrn, P2 tog, yrn, (P1, K1) into last st, make picot.

38th row Cast off 5 sts, yrn, P2 tog, yrn, K8, (yrn, P2 tog) twice, K2, yrn, P2 tog, K2, (yrn, P2 tog) twice, K4, P6, turn, P6, K4, (yrn, P2 tog) twice, K1, K2 tog, yfwd, K3, (yrn, P2 tog) twice, K8, (P1, K1) into next st, yrn, P2 tog, yrn, (P1, K1) into last st, make picot.

39th row Cast off 5sts, yrn, P2 tog, yrn, P3 tog, K7, (yrn, P2 tog) twice, K4, (yrn, P2 tog) 3 times, K4, P5, turn, P5, K4, (yrn, P2 tog) twice, yon, sl 1, K1, psso, K4, (yrn, P2 tog) twice, K6, K2 tog, K1, yrn, P2 tog, yrn, (P1, K1) into last st, make picot.

40th row Cast off 5 sts, yrn, P2 tog, yrn, P3 tog, K5, (yrn, P2 tog) twice, K3, P2 tog tbl, yon, K1, (yrn, P2 tog) twice, K4, P4, turn, P4, K4, (yrn, P2 tog) twice, K2, yfwd, sl 1, K1, psso, K2, (yrn, P2 tog) twice, K4, K2 tog, K1, yrn, P2 tog, yrn, (P1, K1) into last st, make picot.

41st row Cast off 5 sts, yrn, P2 tog, yrn, P3 tog, K3, (yrn, P2 tog) twice, K1, P2 tog tbl, yrn, K3, (yrn, P2 tog) twice, K4, P3, turn, P3, K4, (yrn, P2 tog) twice, K4, yfwd, sl 1, K1, psso, (yrn, P2 tog) twice, K2, K2 tog, K1, yrn, P2, tog, yrn, (P1, K1) into last st, make picot.

42nd row Cast off 5 sts, yrn, P2 tog, yrn, P3 tog, K1, (yrn, P2 tog) 3 times, K4, (yrn, P2 tog) twice, K4, P2, turn, P2, K4, (yrn, P2 tog) twice, K3, K2 tog, yfwd, K1, (yrn, P2 tog)

twice, K2 tog, K1, yrn, P2 tog, yrn, (P1, K1) into last st, make picot.

43rd row Cast off 5 sts, yrn, (P2 tog) twice, (yrn, P2 tog) twice, K2, yrn, P2 tog, Kw, (yrn, P2 tog) twice, K4, P1, turn, P1, K4, (yrn, P2 tog) twice, K1, K2 tog, yfwd, K3, (yrn, P2 tog) twice, sl 1, K2 tog, psso, K1.

44th row K2 tog, (yrn, P2 tog) twice, K4, (yrn, P2 tog) 3 times, K4, turn, K4, (yrn, P2 tog) twice, yon, sl 1, K1, psso, K4, (yrn, P2 tog) twice, K1.

45th row K1, (yrn, P2 tog) twice, K3, P2 tog tbl, yon, K1, (yrn, P2 tog) twice, K4, P20.

46th row P20, K4, (yrn, P2 tog) twice, K2, yfwd, sl 1, K1, psso, K2, (yrn, P2 tog) twice, K1.

47th row K1, (yrn, P2 tog) twice, K1, P2 tog tbl, yon, K3, (yrn, P2 tog) twice, K4, P20.

48th-64th rows Repeat 31st-47th rows inclusive once more.
The last 64 rows form the pattern repeat.
Repeat these 64 rows 4 times more.
Repeat 1st-30th rows once more.
Next 2 rows P.
Cast off very loosely.

To make up

Make a line of running stitches at the neck edge. Gather into the required measurement. Curve the collar, stretch and pin it into shape. Starch and press. Make a button loop (see Making a button loop) at the neck edge. Sew on the button to fasten.

Making a button loop

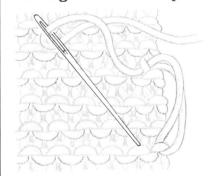

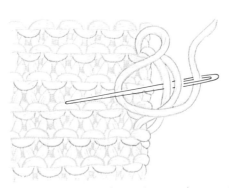

1 Thread a suitable needle with matching yarn. Secure on the wrong side at one end of the loop position. Bring it through to the right side. Make a small stitch at the other end of the loop position then another stitch at the starting point to make a double thread the length of the loop.

2 Make a buttonhole stitch over the double thread by taking the needle from back to front under the thread and winding the yarn round as shown. Tighten the knot.

3 Continue in buttonhole stitch until the thread is completely covered. Secure the end of the yarn at the back of the work.

Chapter 5

Crocheted Lace

Crocheted laces are amazingly varied and adaptable, and surprisingly easy to work. Edgings, for example, can be crocheted directly into fabric, or they can be made separately, either with a pretty edge and applied like any other lace trim, or with straight edges as an insertion. Motifs can be used singly as medallions like the cushion on page 109, or joined together by various linking stitches to form all-over fabric such as the picot mesh of Irish lace (see page 126). Alternatively, linking stitches may be used on their own — with or without picots — to produce beautiful mesh fabrics like the bolster cover on page 110 and the Irish lace T-shirt (page 127).

There is also another form of crocheted lace called tambour work whereby delicate line designs are produced working with a fine steel crochet hook and thread on a net ground. An example of this is the wedding veil given on page 124.

In the following pages, instructions are given for making pretty home-linen trims, cushion covers and tablecloths, shelf edging, and a range of beautiful traditional garments and accessories.

Lace trimmed bed linen

Pretty edgings, worked in white cotton, have been used to decorate
a mid-pink sheet and pillowcase, but you could use bright colours
just as successfully to enhance white bed linen. Worked in medium
cotton, these beautiful wide edgings would look equally good on
other furnishings, such as tablecloths and runners
or pretty clothes.

Materials

These lacy edgings look most effective when worked in a medium-thick, slightly shiny yarn, such as a number 3 or 5 cotton — here the edgings are worked in a number 3 cotton which complements perfectly the treble and double treble stitch patterns used.

Choose colours to match or contrast with the article that you are edging. The choice in some range of cotton may be a little restricted, so if you want to match a colour exactly, use white cotton and, after completing the edging, dip it in a commercial cold-water dye available from most department stores.

Tension

12 pairs of treble on the base measure 10cm in length

Abbreviations

The following abbreviations are used in crochet patterns:

ch	chain
cont	continu(e)(ing)
dc	double crochet
dtr	double treble
htr	half treble
inc	increase
patt	pattern
qtr	quadruple treble
rep	repeat
RS	right side
ss	slip stitch or single crochet
sp(s)	space(s)
tr	treble
tr tr	triple treble
WS	wrong side
yrh	yarn round hook

You will need

To trim one standard single-bed sheet and pillowcase — edging 7cm at widest point:

Two 50g balls of Twilleys Stalite
2.50mm crochet hook

Sheet edging

Base Using 2.50mm hook, make 7ch, 1tr into 6th ch from hook, 1tr into last ch, turn, *5ch, 1tr into each of next 2tr, turn*, rep from * to * for width of sheet, so that total number of 5ch loops on each edge of base is divisible by 4. Work from * to * once more, ss into next tr and into first 3ch of first 5ch loop.

1st row (RS) 1dc into same place as last ss, *4ch, 1dc into next 5ch loop, 1ch, 7tr into next 5ch loop, 1ch, 1dc into next 5ch loop, 4ch, 1dc into next 5ch loop, rep from * to end. Turn.

2th row 1ch, 1dc into first ch, *4dc into next 4ch loop, 1ch (1tr into next tr, 1ch) 7 times, 4dc into next 4ch loop, 1dc into next dc, rep from * to end, ending last rep with 1dc into last dc. Turn.

3rd row 1ch, miss first dc, 1dc into each of next 3dc, *2ch, (1tr into next tr, 1ch) 6 times, 1tr into next tr, 2ch, miss next 2dc into each of next 5dc, rep from * to end, ending last rep with miss next 2dc, 1dc into each of next 3dc. Turn.

4th row 3ch, *(1tr into next tr, 2ch) 7 times, 1dc into 3rd of next 5dc, 2ch, rep from * to end, ending last rep with 1dc into last dc. Turn.

5th row 4ch, *1dtr into next tr, 2ch, (1dtr into next tr, 3ch, ss to top of dtr just worked, 2ch) 5 times, 1dtr into next tr, rep from * to end, 4ch, ss to first of 3 turning ch at beg of 4th row. Fasten off.

Inner edge With RS facing, rejoin yarn to top of first tr on other edge of base, 6ch, *1dc into next 5ch loop, 4ch, rep from * to end, 6ch, ss to base of last tr.
Fasten off.

Pillowcase edging

Work as for Sheet edging, but rep Base from * to * for width of pillowcase.

1st-5th rows and inner edge Work as for Sheet edging.

To make up

Using rustless steel pins, pin out the edging to the correct size and damp lightly. Allow it to dry and then sew it neatly on to the sheet and pillowcase, see Working stab stitch.

Note It is best to remove the edging when laundering. Wash the edging separately from the article and reblock it before reattaching it to the article.

Working stab stitch

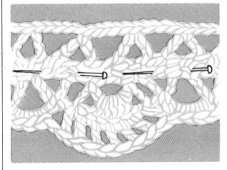

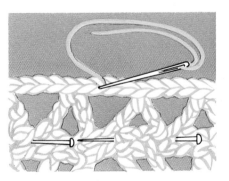

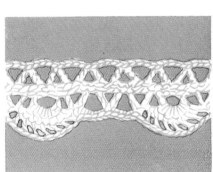

1 Stab stitch is a method of invisibly attaching an edging to an article. After completing the edging, pin and block it to the correct size, lightly damp and allow to dry. Place the edging with right side facing on the front of the article and pin it into position.

2 Using a sharp sewing needle and thread to match the edging, begin with a small double back-stitch on the wrong side. Bring the needle through all thicknesses to the front and then, inserting the needle slightly to the left, push it to the back of the work. Bring it to the front about 5mm to the left.

3 Continue working stab stitch in this way to the end. Finish with a double back-stitch.

Working foundation chain (ch)

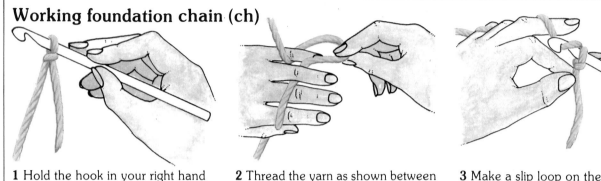

1 Hold the hook in your right hand as if you were holding a pencil.

2 Thread the yarn as shown between the fingers of the left hand so that it flows freely and evenly.

3 Make a slip loop on the hook. Take the yarn over the hook and draw through the loop to make the first chain. After making a few chain, move up your finger and thumb to just below the hook.

Treble crochet (tr)

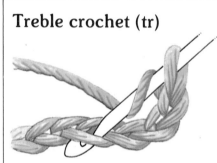

1 Make a chain the length needed. Take the yarn anti-clockwise over the hook. Miss the first three chain and insert the hook from front to back under the top two loops of the fourth chain from the hook. (The three chain missed at the beginning should be counted as the first treble.)

2 Take the yarn anti-clockwise over the hook and draw yarn through the chain — three loops on the hook.

3 Take the yarn anti-clockwise over the hook. Draw the yarn through the first two loops on the hook — two loops remain on the hook.

4 Take the yarn anti-clockwise over the hook. Draw the yarn through the remaining two loops on the hook — one treble has been worked and one loop only remains on the hook.

Double treble (dtr)

1 To work the base row, take the yarn anti-clockwise over the hook **twice** and insert the hook from front to back under the top two loops of the fifth chain from the hook. Take the yarn once over the hook and draw through the first two loops on the hook — three loops remain on the hook.

2 Take the yarn over the hook and draw it through the first two loops on the hook — two loops remain. Take the yarn over the hook and draw it through the remaining two loops on the hook — one loop remains and one double treble has been worked. Continue working double treble in this way into the next and each chain to the end. Turn.

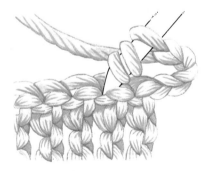

3 At the beginning of the next and every following row, work four turning chain to count as the first double treble. At the end of each row work the last double treble into the top of the four turning chain.

Star-motif tablecloth

Star-shaped motifs are formed by working in the round combining a variety of lacy stitch patterns. Most stars have either six or eight sides, but all can be sewn or crocheted together to make delicate household linen, as in this fine lacy tablecloth which can be made to any size.

Materials

Stars, like many motifs, are best worked in a smooth, crisp yarn so that the crochet retains its shape. Cotton is ideal, though synthetic yarns of the same texture are also suitable. The thickness of the yarn of course governs the eventual size of the motif — the thicker the yarn, the larger the motif.

The tablecloth in the project is formed from motifs worked in number 20 mercerized cotton, but slighly thicker cotton could be used for a chunkier look.

Tension

The small filling motif measures approximately 3.5cm between its widest points, and the large star motif measures 11cm between its widest points

Abbreviations

See page 101

You will need

For a tablecloth where one 20g ball makes 6 large motifs and 6 small filling motifs

Coats Chain Mercer Crochet Cotton, No. 20
1.25 mm crochet hook

First star motif

**Using 1.25mm hook, wind yarn 20 times round tip of little finger to form a circle (see Working an open centre) ss into circle.

1st round 4ch, 3dtr into circle, (3ch, 4dtr into circle) 7 times, 3ch, ss to top of first 4ch. (See page 102 for Working the foundation chain and Double treble stitch.)

2nd round 1ch, 1dc into next dtr, 3ch, ss to last dc worked — picot formed —, 1dc into each of next 2dtr, *(1dc, 3ch, 1dc) into next 3ch sp, 1dc into each of next 2dtr, picot, 1dc into each of next 2dtr, rep from * 7 times more, (1dc, 3ch, 1dc) into next 3ch sp, ss to first ch.

3rd round Ss across first 4dc and into first 3ch sp, 4ch, 1dtr into same 3ch sp, (10ch, work 2dtr tog into next 3ch sp) 7 times, 10ch, ss to top of first 4ch.

4th round 1ch, (13dc into next 10ch sp) 8 times, ss to first ch.

5th round 4ch, miss next dc, (1tr into next dc, 1ch, miss next dc) 51 times, ss to 3rd of first 4ch.

6th round 1ch, (2dc into next 1ch sp) 52 times, ss to first ch.

7th round Ss across first 4dc, (7ch,

miss next 4dc, 1dc into next dc, 10ch, miss next 7dc, 1dc into next dc) 8 times. **

8th round *(4dc, picot, 4dc) into next 7ch loop, 9dc into next 10ch loop, 7ch, ss into 5th of 9dc just worked, (4dc, picot, 4dc) into next 7ch loop, 4dc into remainder of 10ch loop, rep from * to end, ending with ss to first dc.
Fasten off.

Second star motif

Work from ** to ** of First star motif.

8th round (4dc, picot, 4dc) into next 7ch loop, 9dc into next 10ch loop, 7ch, ss into 5th dc of 9dc just worked, (4dc, 1ch, ss to corresponding picot on First star motif, 1ch, 4dc) into next 7ch loop, 4dc into remainder of 10ch loop, complete round as for 8th round of First star motif.

Continue working Second star motifs in this way until tablecloth is the required width.

First filling motif

Begin and work 1st round as for First star motif.

2nd round 1ch, 1dc into next dtr, picot, 1dc into each of next 2dtr, 1dc into next 3ch sp, 1ch, ss to large picot on inner edge of First star motif, 1ch, 1dc into same 3ch sp, 1dc into each of next 2dtr, picot, 1dc into each of next 2dtr, (1dc, 3ch, 1dc) into next 3ch sp, 1dc into each of next 2dtr, picot, 1dc into each of next 2dtr, 1dc into next 3ch sp, 1ch, ss to large picot on inner edge of Second star motif, complete round as for 2nd round of First star motif.
Fasten off.

Continue working Filling motifs in the same way between Large star motifs.

Next star motif row

Work from ** to ** as for First star motif.

8th round *(4ch, picot, 4ch) into next 7ch loop, 9dc into next 10ch loop, 7ch, ss into 5th of 9dc just worked, (4dc, 1ch, ss to corresponding large picot on first motif of previous Star motif row, 1ch, 4dc) into next 7ch loop, 4dc into remainder of 10ch loop *, rep from * to * once, joining 1ch to corresponding 1ch sp on next Filling motif, complete round as for 8th round of First star motif. Work following Large star motifs in the same way, joining each motif to previous Large star motif of this row, Filling motif of previous row, next Large star motif of previous row and next Filling motif of previous row. Continue in this way until the tablecloth is required length, omitting Filling motifs from last row of Large star motifs.

Edging

With RS facing and using 1.25mm hook, join yarn to first picot of corner motif.

1st round 4ch, 1dtr into same picot, 10ch, 1dc into next large picot, (10ch, 1dc into next picot, 10ch, 1dc into next large picot) 4 times, 10ch, work 2dtr tog into last picot of same motif, *work 2dtr tog into first picot of next motif, (10ch, 1dc into next large picot, 10ch, 1dc into next picot) 3 times omitting 1dc at end of last rep, work 2dtr tog into last large picot, rep from * to end, working extra 10ch loops on corner motifs as required, ss to top of first 4ch.

2nd round (7dc, picot, 7dc) into first loop, *9dc into next loop, 7ch, ss into 5th of 9dc just worked, (4dc, picot, 4dc) into next 7ch loop, 4dc into remainder of 10ch loop*, rep from * to * 7 times more, **(7dc, picot, 7dc) into next loop **, rep from ** to ** once more, rep from * to * 4 times more, cont in this way, working extra picot points at each corner as requried, ss to first dc. Fasten off.

To make up

Darn in all ends. Working on a well-padded surface, and using fine rustless pins, pin out the cloth to shape. Secure each picot with a pin. Press tablecloth under a damp cloth.

Working an open centre

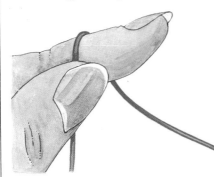 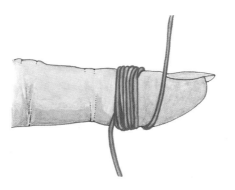 

1 Some motifs worked in the round have a large, open centre. This is sometimes formed from a circle of chain, but a neater method has been used for the motifs in the basic tablecloth. Hold the yarn over the little finger of your left hand about 10cm from the cut end. Hold the ball of yarn in your right hand.

2 Wind the yarn from the ball 20 times around the tip of your little finger. Cover the short end as you wind to secure it and wind firmly but not too tightly so that the resulting circle can be removed easily from your finger.

3 Carefully remove the yarn circle from your finger. Then, holding circle and working yarn in your left hand, use a hook of the required size to work a slip stitch into the circle to prevent it unwinding. Continue to motif as given in the pattern. Then join motifs while working the last rounds.

Note When using thicker yarn, wind the yarn fewer times around your little finger.

Inlaid tablecloth

You can enhance a variety of household items by mastering the simple art of joining crochet motifs to crisp cotton or linen to give an inlaid effect. Here this attractive linen cloth is inlaid and edged with matching motifs worked in fine cotton thread.

Materials

The best results are obtained by using fine or medium-weight crochet cottons for the motifs, since they are firm enough to hold the shape of the motif without being too heavy for the fabric surround. It is important to make sure that the crochet motifs, once they have been joined into strips, are not too heavy for the fabric to be used for the main section, as they could distort the finished article, pulling it out of shape.

For this reason either a good quality, loosely-woven cotton or firm linen are both suitable fabrics since they will hold the crochet motifs firmly. On the other hand, you should not choose a fabric which is so heavy that it will overpower the crochet motifs, thus losing the attractive effect created by combining open lace patterns with solid fabric.

Tension

One motif measures approximately 5cm square

Abbreviations

See page 101

You will need

For a cloth, approximately 60cm square

Three balls of Coats Mercer Crochet No. 20
1.25mm crochet hook
4 pieces of Glenshee linen each approximately 30cm square
Matching sewing thread

1st motif

Wind crochet cotton 12 times round end of pencil, slip off and catch ring together with a ss.
1st round 3ch, 2tr into ring, 7ch, (3tr, 7ch) 7 times into ring. Join with a ss to 3rd of first 3ch.
2nd round Ss across next 2tr and 2ch, 3ch, keeping last loop of each st on hook, work 3tr into first 7ch loop, yrh and through all loops on hook — called 3tr cluster —, (9ch, leaving last loop of each st on hook, work 4tr into next 7ch loop, yrh and through all loops on hook — called 4tr cluster

—,) 7 times, 9ch. Join with a ss to top of first cluster.
3rd round *(2dc, 5ch, 2dc) into next 9ch loop, 7ch, (4tr cluster, 5ch, 4tr cluster) into next 9ch loop, 7ch, rep from * to end of round. Join with a ss to first dc.
4th round Ss into next dc and into 5ch loop, 2dc into same loop, *5ch, 2dc into next 7ch loop, 5ch, (4tr cluster, 5ch, 4tr cluster) into next 5ch loop, 5ch, 2dc into next 7ch loop, 5ch, 2dc into next 5ch loop, rep from * to end of round ending with 5ch, join with a ss to beg of round.
Fasten off.

2nd motif

Work first 3 rounds as for first motif.
4th round (joining round) Ss into next dc and into 5ch loop, 2dc into same loop, 5ch, 2dc into next 7ch loop, 5ch, 4tr cluster into next 5ch loop, 2ch, ss to corner 5ch loop of **1st motif**, 2ch, 4tr cluster into same 5ch loop of **2nd motif**, (2ch, ss to next loop of **1st motif**, 2ch, 2dc into next loop of **2nd motif**) 3 times, 2ch, ss into next loop of **1st motif**, 2ch, 4tr cluster into next loop of **2nd motif**, 2ch, ss into corner loop of **1st motif**, 2ch, 4tr cluster into same loop of **2nd motif**.
Now complete 2nd motif as given for first motif.
Cont working motifs in this way, joining each motif while working the last round.
Work one strip of 11 motifs and 2 strips of 5 motifs each.
Join these strips to form a cross.

To make up

Press both the linen and crochet under a damp cloth, pinning crochet out to shape before pressing.

Lace edging

1st round With RS of work facing, join yarn to dc at any corner, 3ch, 3tr cluster into same dc as join, 5ch, 4tr cluster into next dc, *5ch, miss 50mm along edge, 1dc into each of next 2dc, 5ch, miss 50mm along edge, 4tr cluster into next dc, 5ch,

Edging the fabric

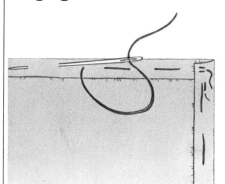 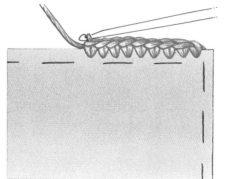 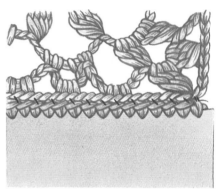

1 Turn a single hem to the wrong side of the fabric all round and tack it into place, making sure that each piece of linen measures 26cm square. Clip the corners diagonally if you are using thick fabric.

2 With RS of the linen facing, insert the fine hook firmly through both layers of fabric and work double crochet closely along the edge of the material, working from right to left and making sure that the stitches are worked evenly so that the fabric is not pulled out of shape. When the hems have been completed cut away the excess fabric on the WS.

3 With the RS of the linen facing, sew the motifs along the edge to the double crochet edging, using a matching sewing thread and holding the crochet and fabric side by side to ensure a flat join.

4tr cluster into next dc, rep from * ending with 2dc at corner before motif. Work across motif as follows: 5ch, miss corner loop of motif, (4tr cluster, 5ch, 4tr cluster) into next loop, (5ch, 2dc into next loop) twice, 5ch, (4tr cluster, 5ch, 4tr cluster) into next loop, 5ch, 2dc into corner of next square of cloth, 5ch, cont in patt to match edging already worked. Join final 5ch to top of 1st cluster with a ss.
2nd round Ss into 5ch loop, 3ch, 3tr cluster into same loop, 5ch, 4tr cluster into same loop, * (5ch, 2dc

into next loop) twice, 5ch, (4tr cluster, 5ch, 4tr cluster) into next loop, rep from * all round cloth but working an extra 5ch loop at centre of motif to keep patt correct.
Join final 5ch to top of 1st cluster with a ss.
Fasten off.
Press completed cloth on WS under a damp cloth.

Note Washing may cause crochet to fall out of shape. Pin the cloth to correct size and press firmly under a damp cloth.

Above: Insertion motif. This lends a delicate, lacy effect to the cloth

Right: Cushion motif. Choose two or three colours to suit your interior scheme.

Medallion cushion

With a combination of crochet and sewing skills you can make a multitude of different inlaid crochet designs. The motif here has been set on a contrasting fabric to that used for the rest of the cushion to show off the crochet work to its best advantage.

Tension
The motif measures 14cm in diameter

Abbreviations
See page 101

You will need
For a cushion cover, 36cm by 36cm

One 20g ball each of Twilley's Lystwist rayon in main colour (A) and a contrast colour (B)
2.50mm crochet hook
Two 37cm squares of linen
35cm-square cushion pad
50cm of contrast fabric
1.50m of piping cord

Front of cushion cover
Crochet one two-colour rosette using colours A and B as follows:
Using A, wind yarn 20 times round tip of little finger. Catch the ring tog with a ss.

1st round Work 24dc into ring. Join with a ss to beg of round.
2nd round (20ch, miss 1dc, 1dc into each of next 2dc) 8 times. Join with a ss to beg of round. Fasten off.
3rd round Using A, join yarn to centre of any 20ch loop, 2dc into same loop, (10ch, 2dc into next loop) 7 times, 10ch. Join with a ss to beg of round.
4th round Ss into next dc and into 10ch loop, 3ch, 15tr into same loop, (16tr into next loop) 7 times.
5th round (1dc into first st of next group, 1tr in each of next 14tr, 1dc into last st of group) 8 times. Join with ss to beg of round. Fasten off.
6th round Using B, work as for 5th round.
7th round Work (2 loose dc inserting hook into space beween trebles of 4th round, 1tr into each of next 14tr) 8 times. Join with a ss to beg of round. Fasten off.
Locate centre of linen square by folding it diagonally both ways.
Using compasses and HB pencil mark a circle of 5.5cm radius in the centre of fabric.
On contrast fabric mark and cut out a 5.5cm-radius circle and place over the circle marked on the main square.
Tack in position.
Then machine stitch with a zigzag stitch or hand sew in buttonhole stitch.
Place the motif centrally over the contrast fabric so that the petals overlap the linen. Attach the motif with small running stitches around the petal edges.
Cut piping strips from contrast fabric. Cover sufficient piping cord and attach piping around the fabric cover edges.
Make up the cushion cover securing the piping within the seam. Insert a square cushion pad and finish off neatly.

Bolster cushion cover

This simple cushion cover is made from one rectangular piece of honeycomb lace fabric seamed to form a tube. The cords, decorated with delicate tassels, make drawstring ties at each end for easy removal of the cushion pad.

Materials

This pretty honeycomb lace is made up of alternating lacets horizontally as well as vertically. Used as a furnishing fabric, this stitch looks most attractive when it is worked in fine to medium cotton — with or without a shiny surface. The rows can be turned either with a straight edge or with a looped edge. Use honeycomb stitch with a looped edge when the fabric is to be gathered with a cord or ribbon, and with a straight edge when the sides of the fabric are to be seamed. The spaces in the pattern can be used most effectively for threading through ribbons or for drawstring ties.

Tension

10 rows to 5cm over pattern.

Abbreviations

See page 101

You will need

For a bolster cushion cover, to fit a cushion pad approximately 45cm long, and 17cm in diameter

Six 20g balls of Coats Mercer Crochet Cotton No. 10
2mm crochet hook
Cushion pad, 45cm long by 17cm diameter
Piece of card 9cm long

Honeycomb stitch with looped edge

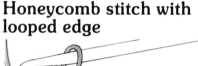

1 Make a foundation chain, miss the 1st 5 chain and work 1 treble into the 6th chain from the hook. *Make 3 chain, miss 3 of the foundation chain, work 1 treble into the next foundation chain, make 2 chain, miss another foundation chain, work 1 double crochet into the next foundation chain, make 2 chain, miss another foundation chain, work 1 treble into the next foundation chain. Repeat from * all along the row.

2 Turn to begin the next row by working 5 chain. Make 1 treble into the 1st treble on the previous row, *make 3 chain then 1 treble into the next treble, 2 chain, 1 double crochet into the 3-chain loop on the previous row, 2 chain, 1 treble into the next treble, repeat from * to the end of the row. Repeat this row to form pattern.

Honeycomb stitch with straight edge

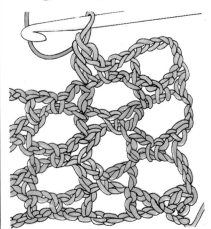

Turn each row with 6 chain instead of 5. Omit the 1st treble and following 3 chain of each row so that the 6 chain take their place.

Chain cord

1 Tie two threads together to form a slip knot placed on the crochet hook. Wind one thread round the fingers of the left hand as for crochet, and the other thread round the right hand as for knitting.

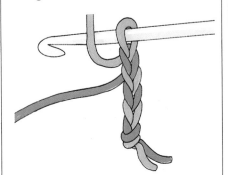

2 Make a chain, using each thread alternately. Tighten each chain stitch after working to maintain an even tension.

Cushion cover

Make 205ch.
1st row 1tr into 6th ch from hook, *3ch, miss next 3ch, 1tr into foll ch, 2ch, miss next ch, 1dc into foll ch, 2ch, miss next ch, 1tr into foll ch, rep from * to end, turn.
2nd row 5ch, 1tr into first tr, *3ch, 1tr into next tr, 2ch, 1dc into 3ch loop, 2ch, 1tr into next tr, rep from * to end, turn.
Rep 2nd row until work measures 58cm, or size required, ending with a 2nd row so that the alt lacets follow through to make a neat join.

Chain cord

Cut four lengths of thread each 3m long and use two on each hand to make a chain cord. (See Making a chain cord.)
Make a similar second cord.

Making a tassel cap

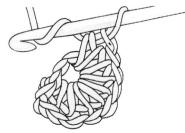

1 Make 7 chain and form a ring by joining into the 1st chain with a slip stitch. Make 2 more chain. Inserting the hook into the centre of the ring, work 10 half treble. Complete the round by joining with a slip stitch to the 2 chain at the beginning.

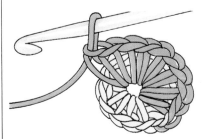

2 Cover the round of half treble with a round of 14 double crochet, again inserting the hook into the centre of the ring for each stitch and drawing each stitch out to make it long enough to go over the half treble. The double crochet is shown here in contrast for clarity.

Tassels

Wind the yarn 60 times around the 9cm piece of card. Cut through the loops at one edge of the card to make the lengths for each tassel. Secure the lengths at the centre and fold in half. For making and fitting the tassel caps, see Making a tassel cap.

To make up

Join the long seam of the cover to make a tube. Thread one cord through the loops at each end as shown. Slip a tassel cap on to each cord end, sew centre of tassel lengths to the cord and slip the cap into place over the head of the tassel.
Place the cushion pad inside the cover and pull the cords tight and tie them in bows at each end to secure.

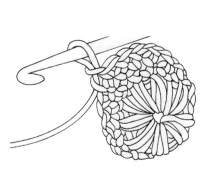

3 Make a cup shape by working 1 double crochet in the usual way into each of the 14 double crochet. At the end of the round do not join with a slip stitch to the first of the round, but continue to work seven rounds of double crochet to form a spiral.
Make a final ss and fasten off.
Make three more tassels.

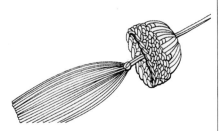

4 Cut lengths of thread to form the tassel. Tie the threads at the centre, fold them in half and slip the cap over the looped end, passing the tie through the centre of the cap.

Lacy shelf edging

Revive a Victorian tradition and trim your cupboard or dresser shelves with this pretty pointed edging — or you may prefer to decorate items of clothing or household linen.

Before you begin

The attractive appearance of this diagonal lace edging is due to the large increases repeating along one side, which alter the direction of the rows, making them run at an angle of 45° instead of running horizontally in the usual way.

The solid part of the edging is made of trebles which form a triangular shape, and the lace part is basically a two-row pattern built up from trebles, double crochet and chains (see page 102, 115). All these stitches are worked together to build up this edging.

Materials

Fine crochet cottons, or alternatively, linen and even synthetic threads of a similar thickness, are most suitable for working delicate lacy trims. For a more contemporary look, plain or variegated colours would look equally stunning.

Tension

One repeat of the pattern measures 6cm

Abbreviations

See page 101

You will need

For an edging, 8cm deep at the widest point

One ball of Coats Mercer Crochet No. 20 for every 106cm of edging
1.25cm crochet hook

To make the lace edging

See: Beginning the edging and Working the lace stitch.
Start with 13ch.
1st row Miss 9ch, 1tr into each of following 4ch, turn.
2nd row 3ch, miss 1st tr, 1tr into each of next 3tr, 4tr into 9ch loop, turn.
3rd row 9ch, 1tr into 1st tr, 1tr into each of next 6tr, 1tr into top of 3ch at

end, turn.

4th row 3ch, miss 1st tr, 1tr into each of next 7tr, 4tr into 9ch loop, turn.

5th row 9ch, 1tr into 1st tr, 1tr into each of next 10tr, 1tr into top of 3ch at end, turn.

6th row 3ch, miss 1st tr, 1tr into each of next 11tr, 4tr into 9ch loop, turn.

7th row 9ch, 1tr into 1st tr, 1tr into each of next 14tr, 1tr into top of 3ch at end, turn.

8th row 3ch, miss 1st tr, 1tr into each of next 15tr, 4tr into 9ch loop, turn.

9th row 9ch, 1tr into 1st tr, 1tr into each of next 3tr, *4ch, miss 3tr, (1tr, 2ch, 1tr) into next tr. Repeat from * 3 times more, counting the 3ch at the end as the last tr, turn.

10th row 5ch, *(1tr, 2ch) 3 times into 2ch space, 1dc into 4ch space, 2ch. Repeat from * 3 times more, 1tr into each of next 4tr, 4tr into 9ch loop, turn.

12th row 5ch, *(1tr, 2ch) 3 times into 2ch space, 1dc into 4ch space, 2ch. Repeat from * 3 times more, 1tr into each of next 8tr, 4tr into 9ch loop, turn.

13th row 9ch, 1tr into 1st tr, 1tr into each of next 11tr, *4ch, (1tr, 2ch, 1tr) into 2nd tr of next group. Repeat from * 3 times more, turn.

14th row 5ch, *(1tr, 2ch) 3 times into 2ch space, 1dc into 4ch space, 2ch. Repeat from * 3 times more, 1tr into each of next 12tr, 4tr into 9ch loop, turn.

15th row 9ch, 1tr into 1st tr, 1tr into each of next 15tr, * 4ch, (1tr, 2ch, 1tr) into 2nd tr of next group. Repeat from * 3 times more, turn.

16th row 5ch, * (1tr, 2ch) 3 times into 2ch space, 1dc into 4ch space, 2ch. Repeat from * 3 times more, 1tr into each of next 16tr, 4tr into 9ch loop, turn.

Repeat 9th to 16th rows, inclusive, for length required. Finish off. Press under a damp cloth before attaching to the shelves with touch and close tape, spaced at regular intervals around the outer edge.

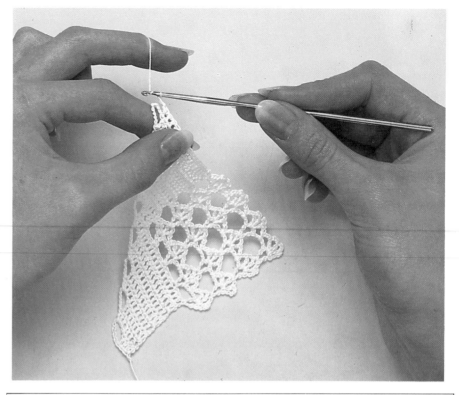

Beginning the edging

1 Start with 13 chain, miss the first 9 chain and work 1 treble into each of the remaining 4 chain.

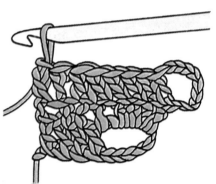

3 Turn and work 9 chain, 1 treble into the first treble, 1 treble into each remaining treble, and 1 treble into the top of the 3 chain at the end which counts as the last treble.

2 *Turn work and begin the next row with 3 chain, miss the first treble, work 1 treble into each remaining treble, then work 4 treble into the loop made by the missed 9 chain.

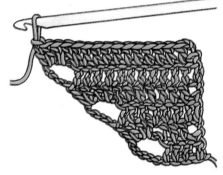

4 Repeat from * until there are 16 trebles in the row. The 9 chain loops form increases at the left-hand side which now becomes the bias inner face of the lace edging.

Working the lace stitch

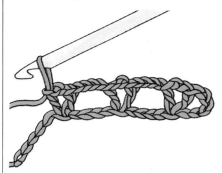

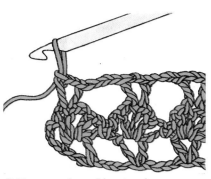

1 Make a number of foundation chain divisible by 5, plus 1 more. Miss the first 5 chain and work (1 treble, 2 chain, 1 treble) all into the 6th chain, *work 4 chain and miss the next 4 foundation chain, work (1 treble, 2 chain, 1 treble) all into the 5th chain. Repeat from * all along.

3 Turn work and begin the next row with 5 chain, then work * (1 treble, 2 chain, 1 treble) all into the second treble of the 3 treble group. Work 4 chain. Repeat from * all along, omitting the final 4 chain.

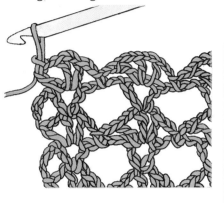

2 Turn work and begin the next row with 5 chain, work * (1 treble, 2 chain, 1 treble, 2 chain, 1 treble, 2 chain) all into the next 2 chain space of the previous row. Work 1 double crochet into the 4 chain space, followed by 2 chain. Repeat from * omitting the final 2 chain and 1 double crochet.

4 Repeat steps 2 and 3 to make the basic lace stitch. In the edging given in the project this is used in conjunction with rows of solid trebles.

Double crochet (dc)

1 To work the base row, miss the first of the foundation chain and insert the hook from front to back under the top two loops of the second chain from the hook. Take the yarn over the hook and draw through a loop — two loops on the hook.

2 Take the yarn over the hook and draw it through the two loops on the hook — one loop remains and one double crochet has been worked. Work one double crochet into the next and every foundation chain, then turn over the work as you would a page in a book.

3 To begin the next row, work one turning chain to count as the first stitch. Miss the last stitch of the previous row and work one double crochet into every following stitch, working the last double crochet into the turning chain of the previous row. Repeat for double crochet fabric.

Left: Using very fine cotton, you can also work diagonal edging to trim delicate lingerie or bedlinen.

Lacy collar and cuffs

These delicate lacy collar and cuffs would look pretty on a fine wool sweater or dress. Make them in a colour to match or contrast with accessories for a special occasion.

Before you begin

Even the simplest of lace stitches — double crochet, treble, double treble, chains, and slipstitch — can be arranged in various combinations to form intriguing pattern repeats, as seen here in this classic collar and cuffs set. Their visual appeal frequently depends more on the spaces left between the stitches than on the stitches themselves.

Most suitable threads for working the collar and cuffs are fine cottons or lightweight wool yarns. An alternative to the conventional foundation chain, called a spaced 'chain', is used in the project. It is much easier to count, and much easier to work into afterwards.

Tension

71 sps of foundation ch on collar measures 48cm. 31 sps of foundation ch on cuffs measures 20cm

Abbreviations

See page 101

You will need

For a collar, 48cm long by 6.5cm wide, and cuffs, 20cm long by 6.5cm wide

One 20g ball of Coats Mercer Crochet Cotton No. 20
1.25mm crochet hook
2m narrow ribbon

Collar

See: Working a spaced chain.
Using a 1.25mm hook, start with 4ch, 1dtr into 4th ch from hook, * 4ch, 1 dtr into sp between previous 4ch and dtr, rep from * until there are 71 sps, turn.
1st row * 9ch, 1dc into next sp. Rep from * to end, turn. (71 loops.)
2nd row 5ch, (2tr, 2ch, 2tr) into first 9ch loop, * (3ch, 1dc into next loop) 9 times, 3ch, (2tr, 2ch, 4tr, 2ch, 2tr) into next loop, rep from * to end, finishing with (2tr, 2ch, 2tr) into last loop, turn.
3rd row 3ch, * (2tr, 2ch, 2tr) into 2ch sp, 3ch, mis first 3ch loop, (1dc into next 3ch loop, 3ch) 8 times, miss 3ch loop, (2tr, 2ch, 2tr) into next 2ch sp, 5ch, rep from * to end, finishing

with (2tr, 2ch, 2tr) into last 2ch sp, turn.
4th row 3ch, * (2tr, 2ch, 2tr) into 2ch sp, 3ch, mis first 3ch loop, (1dc into next 3ch loop, 3ch) 7 times, miss 3ch loop, (2tr, 2ch, 2tr) into 2ch sp, 5ch, 1dc into 5ch loop, 5ch, rep from * to end, finishing with (2tr, 2ch, 2tr) into last 2ch sp, turn.
5th row 3ch, * (2tr, 2ch, 2tr) into 2ch sp, 3ch, miss first 3ch loop. (1dc into next 3ch loop, 3ch) 6 times, miss 3ch loop, (2tr, 2ch, 2tr) into 2ch sp, 5ch, (1dc into next 5ch loop, 5ch) twice, rep from * to end, finishing with 2tr, 2ch, 2tr) into last 2ch sp, turn.

6th row As 5th, but work (1dc into next 3ch loop, 3ch) 5 times instead of 6, and work (1dc into next 5ch loop, 5ch) 3 times instead of twice.
7th row As 5th, but work (1dc into next 3ch loop, 3ch) 4 times, and work (1dc into next 5ch loop, 5ch) 4 times.
8th and 9th rows Cont in this way keeping the sequence of the patt correct.
10th row 3ch, * (2tr, 2ch, 2tr) into 2ch sp, 3ch, miss first 3ch loop, 1dc into next 3ch loop, 3ch, miss next 3ch loop, (2tr, 2ch, 2tr) into 2ch sp, 5ch, (1dc into next 5ch loop, 5ch) 7 times, rep from * to end finishing

with (2tr, 2ch, 2tr) into 2ch sp, turn.
11th row 3ch, * (2tr, 2ch, 2tr) into 2ch sp, (2tr, 2ch, 2tr) into next 2ch sp, (7ch, 1dc into next 5ch sp) 8 times, 7ch, rep from * to end, finishing with (2tr, 2ch, 2tr) into last 2ch sp, turn.
12th row 7ch, miss first 2ch sp, 1dc into next 2ch sp, * (7ch, 1dc into next loop) 9 times, (7ch, 1dc into 2ch sp) twice, rep from * to end of row, then cont down side of collar, 7ch, (1dc into next 3ch loop, 9ch) 5 times, 1dc into 9ch loop of first row. Fasten off.

Join thread to opposite side of collar and complete to match.

Cuffs
Work as given for collar, making 31 sps only for the foundation, and 31 loops for the first row.

To make up
Block the collar and cuffs to shape in the following way:
Wash the finished crochet if soiled and while still wet, pin each piece out on a padded surface. Use plenty of pins — one in each loop all round the outside — and pull the crochet accurately into shape. Leave until it is quite dry before removing the pins.
If the work does not need to be washed, pin it out dry and spray with water from a spray bottle instead, and leave to dry.
Thread ribbon in and out through the 9ch loops of the first row. Attach it to the garment by sewing through the foundation 'chain'.

Working a spaced 'chain'

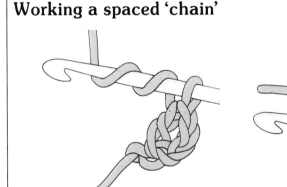

1 Commence with 4 chain, then work 1 double treble into the first of the 4 chain.

2 Make 4 more chain, then work 1 double treble inserting the hook into the space between the double treble and 4 chain previously made.

3 Repeat from * to make a 'chain' consisting of linked spaces. When working the next row, insert the hook into the actual spaces.

Working the basic lace net

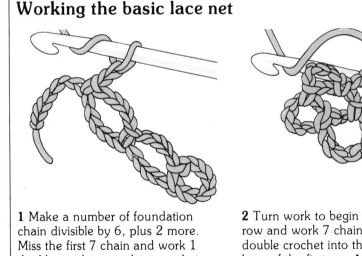

1 Make a number of foundation chain divisible by 6, plus 2 more. Miss the first 7 chain and work 1 double crochet into the next chain, * then work 5 chain, miss 5 chain of the foundation, work 1 double crochet into the next chain. Repeat from * all along the foundation chain to make the first row of net.

2 Turn work to begin the second row and work 7 chain, then work 1 double crochet into the first 5 chain loop of the first row * work 5 chain, then 1 double crochet into the 5 chain loop. Repeat from * all along the row, working the last double crochet into the 7 chain loop at the end. Keep repeating this row to build up the basic lace net.

Tasselled scarf

This neatly edged triangle of silken net can also be draped as a shawl. The tassel adds a pleasing touch of frivolity.

Before you begin

The trebles featured in this particular net stretch the mesh into a honeycomb shape. There are two methods of forming the mesh as the trebles can be worked either into the spaces made by the chain loops, or they can be worked into the centre stitch of each chain loop. The latter method is slower but gives a well shaped mesh. Each method is easy to work but care is needed in turning the rows when shaping.

Tension

9 loops to 10cm

Abbreviations

See page 101

You will need

For a scarf, 120cm wide across the top edge, and 100cm deep at the centre back

19 cones Silverknit Ideal, (1711)
3mm crochet hook

Scarf

See: Working the basic treble net and Shaping a triangle in treble net.
Start with a foundation of 8ch, 1dtr into 8th ch from hook, turn.
1st row 8ch, (1tr, 3ch, 1dtr) into foundation triangle, turn.
2nd row 8ch, 1tr into first loop, 3ch, (1tr, 3ch, 1dtr) into last loop, turn.
3rd row 8ch, 1tr into first loop, 3ch, 1tr into next loop, 3ch, (1tr, 3ch, 1dtr) into last loop, turn.
4th row 8ch, 1tr into first loop, 3ch, (1tr into next loop, 3ch) twice, (1tr, 3ch, 1dtr) into last loop, turn.
5th row 8ch, 1tr into first loop, 3ch, (1tr into next loop, 3ch) 3 times, (1tr, 3ch, 1dtr) into last loop, turn.
Cont in this way until a total of 100 rows have been worked. Do not finish off but cont down side edge.

Side edging

See: Working edging on a triangle.
2ch, 1dc into first loop, 2ch, * (2tr, 2ch, 2tr) into next loop, 2ch, 1dc into following loop, 2ch. Rep from * until lower corner is reached. Rep the pattern again into this loop to ease corner, and cont edging on opposite

Shaping a triangle in treble net

1 Commence with 8 chain, then work a double treble into the first chain made, thus forming a triangle.

2 Turn the work sideways and continue with 8 chain, 1 treble into the top of triangle, 3 chain, and 1 double treble also worked into the triangle.

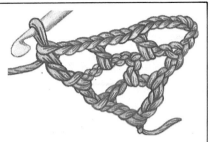

3 Turn the work again and continue with 8 chain, 1 treble into the 3 chain loop, 3 chain, 1 treble into the last loop, 3 chain and 1 double treble also into the last loop.

4 Turn with 8 chain, 1 treble into the first loop, 3 chain, 1 treble into the next loop, 3 chain, (1 treble, 3 chain and 1 double treble) into the last loop. Continue in this way, always starting and ending each row as given.

Working edging on a triangle

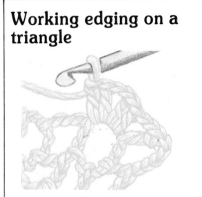

1 When the triangle is the required size, work down side of rows with 2 chain and 1 double crochet, placing the hook into the loop formed by the side of the last double treble. Work 2 more chain. Into the side of the loop formed by the 8 turning chain work 2 treble, 2 chain and 2 treble.

2 Continue with 2 chain, 1 double crochet into the loop formed by the next double treble, 2 chain, (2 treble, 2 chain, 2 treble) into the next loop, and so on.

side to match. Do not finish off but cont for ties and top edging.

Top edging
1st row work 40ch, 1dc into each of 40ch, 3dc into each loop across top of scarf, 40ch, turn.
2nd row 1dc into each of 40ch, 1dc into each dc to end, turn.
3rd row 1dc into each dc, finish off.

Tassel
Cut 30 pieces of yarn 36cm long, fold them in half and loop through the lower corner of the scarf to form a tassel. Trim ends neatly.
Stretch and enlarge the finished work by pinning it out to a floor carpet which has been covered by a cloth. Damp the crochet with a spray of water and leave it until dry. Do not press with an iron, or the body and texture of the yarn will be spoilt.

Working the basic treble net

1 Make a number of chain divisible by 4 plus 1. Work 1 treble into the 5th chain from hook, * 3 chain, miss 3 chain, 1 treble into next chain. Repeat from * to end, turn. Begin the second row with 4 chain, 1 treble into the first loop, * 3 chain, 1 treble into next loop. Repeat from * to end, turn.

2 Repeat the second row to build up basic treble net. Each row begins with a half mesh. To increase in the middle of a row work (3 chain, 1 treble) twice into the same loop.

Mesh gloves

Mesh fabrics are formed from simple repeating patterns and are ideal for delicate openwork garments like these cotton gloves. Although they are not easy to work, the results are well worth a little perseverance.

Materials
When working mesh patterns, choose the yarn most suitable for the article you intend to make. A fine cotton is ideal for garments like the mesh gloves, which were worked in a number 20 cotton. When working small articles, exact tension is vital so if you are unsure about working with cotton, work a sample in your chosen thread first.

Tension
6 Solomon's knots to 5cm worked on 1.25mm hook

Abbreviations
See page 101

You will need
For gloves, to fit the average hand
Note These gloves will stretch to fit most women's hands; washing will restore them to their original size.

Two 20g balls of Twilley's Twenty
1.25mm crochet hook
Tubular elastic to fit round wrists

Right-hand glove
Join length of elastic to fit round wrist. Using 1.25mm hook, work 100dc over elastic, ss to first dc.
1st round * 1 Solomon's knot (see Working Solomon's knot) called 1 SK —, miss next 4dc, 1dc into next dc, rep from * 19 times more.
2nd round * 1 SK, inserting hook under 2 top loops only work 1dc into next SK of last round — called 1dc top —, rep from * to end.
Last round forms SK patt.
Shape base of thumb
3rd round As 2nd round.
4th round (1 SK, 1dc top) twice into next SK — 1 SK inc —, * 1 SK, 1dc top into next SK, rep from * to end.
5th round As 2nd round.
6th round (1 SK, 1dc top) twice into first SK, (1 SK, 1dc top) twice into 2nd SK, *1 SK, 1dc top into next SK, rep from * to end.
7th round As 2nd round.
8th round (1 SK, 1dc top) twice into first SK, mark this inc with a coloured thread, (1 SK, 1dc top into next SK)

4 times, (1 SK, 1dc top) twice into next SK, * 1 SK, 1dc top into next SK, rep from * to end.
9th-13th rounds As 2nd round.
Divide for thumb
14th round Work to position directly above marked inc, 3 SK, miss next 7 SK, 1dc top into next SK, mark last st with a coloured thread, * 1 SK, 1dc top into next SK, rep from * to end.
15th-20th rounds As 2nd. 20 SK.
Divide for first finger
21st round Work to position directly above marked st, 2 SK, miss next 13 SK, 1dc top into next SK.
First finger
Next round (1 SK, 1dc, top into next SK) 8 times.
Cont in rounds of SK patt on these 8 SK until finger measures 7.5cm from beg or length required.

Next round 1ch, (1dc top into next SK, 1ch) 8 times.
Next round 1dc into each of next 8dc. Fasten off, leaving an end of yarn approx 20cm long.
Thread yarn through last round and pull tightly to gather.
Secure yarn and cut off close to sts.
Second finger
Next round With palm facing, rejoin yarn to dc at base of first finger, (1 SK, 1dc top into next SK) twice, 2 SK, miss next 9 SK of last round of palm, 1dc top into next SK, (1 SK, 1dc top into next SK) twice, (1 SK, 1dc top into base of first finger) twice.
Cont in rounds of SK patt on these 8 SK until finger measures 8cm from beg or length required.
Complete as for first finger.
Third finger
Next round With palm facing, rejoin yarn to dc at base of 2nd finger, (1 SK, 1dc top into next SK) twice, 2 SK, miss next 5 SK, 1dc top into next SK, (1 SK, 1dc top into next SK) twice, (1 SK, 1dc top into base of 2nd finger) twice.
Cont in rounds of SK patt on these 8 SK until finger measures 7.5cm from beg or length required.
Complete as for first finger.
Fourth finger
Next round With palm facing, rejoin

yarn to dc at base of 3rd finger, (1 SK, 1dc top into next SK) 5 times, (1 SK, 1dc top into base of 3rd finger) twice.
Cont in rounds of SK patt on these 7 SK until finger measures 7cm from beg or length required.
Next round 1ch, (1dc top into next SK, 1ch) 7 times.
Next round 1dc into each of next 7dc. Fasten off and complete as for first finger.
Thumb
Next round With RS facing, rejoin yarn to dc at right of thumb opening, (1SK, 1dc top into next SK) 7 times, (1 SK, 1dc into next dc) 3 times across back of thumb opening, (1 SK, 1dc top into next SK) 7 times, 1dc top into next SK, miss next SK — 1 SK dec.
Cont in rounds of SK patt on these 9 SK until thumb measures 6cm from beg or length required.
Next round 1ch, (1dc top into next SK, 1ch) 9 times.
Next round 1dc in each of next 9dc. Fasten off. Complete as for first finger.

Cuff
See: Making an elasticated cuff.
Turn glove upside-down and, with RS facing, rejoin yarn to elastic between any 2dc worked over elastic.
1st round Work 100dc over elastic, inserting hook between previous dc.
2nd round (2 SK, miss next 3dc, 1dc into each of next 2dc) 20 times.
3rd round (2 SK, 1dc into knot between 2 SK) 20 times.
4th-6th rounds As 3rd round.
7th round * 1 SK, 7dc into knot between next 2 SK, rep from * to end, ss to first SK. Fasten off.

Left-hand glove
Work palm, fingers and thumb as for right-hand glove, then turn work inside-out.
Work cuff as for right-hand glove.

To make up
Darn in all ends invisibly and cut close to sts. Spray gloves lightly with water and leave to dry naturally. Lightly spray cuffs with starch.

Working Solomon's knot

Solomon's knot can be worked with or without a foundation chain, depending on whether a firm edge is needed. It can be difficult to work, so some practice is advisable.

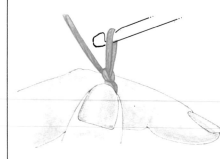

1 Make a slip loop as normal on the hook. Make one chain. Extend the loop on the hook to between 7mm and 13mm depending on the yarn — the thicker the yarn, the longer the loop.

2 Holding the extended loop between the thumb and first finger of the left hand, wind the yarn round the hook and extend the yarn to the same height as the loop. Yarn round hook and draw through a loop.

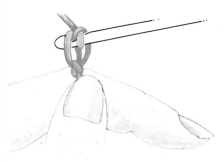

3 Insert the hook from right to left under the vertical loop formed in step 2. Yarn round hook and draw through a loop.

4 Wind the yarn round the hook and draw through both loops to complete the first Solomon's knot. Continue in this way ending with a multiple of two knots plus two.

5 To begin the next row, insert the hook into the fifth knot from the hook and work a double crochet in the normal way. Always work into the centre of each knot to ensure that the knots are joined firmly.

6 Work two more knots, miss the next knot and work a double crochet into the centre of the next knot. Continue in this way working the last double crochet into the chain worked in step 1. Turn.

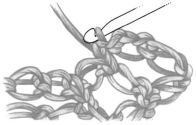

7 Begin every following row with three knots, then work a dc into next knot left unworked in the previous row. Make two knots; work one dc into the next unworked knot. Continue in this way working the last dc into next unworked knot.

Working into a chain

1 To work a Solomon's knot fabric with a firm edge, begin with a multiple of five chain. Extend the loop on the hook and work one knot. Slip stitch into the tenth chain from the hook.

2 Make one chain and work two knots. Miss the next four foundation chain and slip stitch into the next chain. Continue in this way to the end, working the last slip stitch into the last chain. Turn.

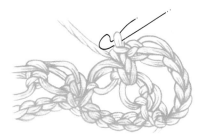

3 Begin every following row with six chain and one knot. Work a double crochet into the next unworked knot of the previous row.

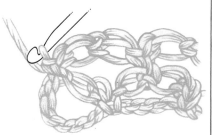

4 Work two knots and then a double crochet into the next un-worked knot. Continue in this way, working the final double crochet into the turning chain of the previous row.

Making an elasticated cuff

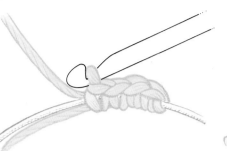
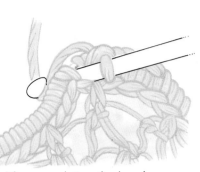

1 Cut a length of tubular elastic to fit comfortably round your wrist plus 5mm. Do not stretch the elastic or the cuff will be too tight.
Overlap the two ends of elastic by 5mm and join with small stitches to form a circle. Secure the stitches and cut the thread close to the elastic.

2 Hold the elastic and yarn between the first finger and thumb. Insert the hook under the elastic, wind the yarn round the hook and draw through a loop. Complete the double crochet as normal. Work 99 more double crochet over the elastic, at the same time working over the end of yarn. Join to the first double crochet with a slip stitch.

3 After completing the hand section, turn the work upside-down and return to the double crochet in step 2.
Insert the hook under the elastic between any two double crochet. Wind the yarn round the hook, draw through a loop and complete the double crochet as normal. Work 99 more double crochet between double crochet and continue in cuff pattern.

Wedding veil

The techniques of tambour work can be used when working crochet on to a net base to form the most delicate of garments, such as this simple yet beautiful wedding veil.

Materials

Tambour crochet is best worked into fine fabrics such as dress-weight nets, muslin, tulle, chiffon, organdie and other sheers. These may be made from either cotton, silk or synthetic fibres. However, the chosen fabric should be fairly loosely woven to allow the hook and thread to pass easily through. Fine steel hooks between 0.60-100mm and 40-60 cotton or similar yarn, are recommended.

You will need

For a veil, 110cm in diameter
1.5m by 1.35m of cream tulle (with about 15 holes to 2cm down and 11 holes to 2cm across)

4 reels of cream silk sewing thread
1 reel of cream machine embroidery thread No. 50
Large slate frame or tambour hoop (with stand)
1.00mm crochet hook

To make

First mark the circumference of the veil. To do this, fold the net into quarters, finger press the crease lines and open out flat. Tack along the fold lines to give four quarters. Then, hold one end of a measuring tape firmly in the centre of the net, and using pins, mark a 55cm radius all round, placing the pins between 3cm-4cm apart. Mark the outline with tacking stitches and remove the pins. Do not cut away the surrounding net.

Enlarge the design given below (which is a quarter of the full pattern) to the required size, where one square equals ten centimetres. Work directly on to good quality tracing paper and go over the outlines with a black felt pen. This means that, when transferring the design to net, the tracing can be reversed for each quarter section.

Place the net over the design matching the centre lines, and pin to hold. Lightly transfer the outline with tailor's chalk. Remove the pins. Stretch the net in the embroidery frame. For those lines of the design indicated in red, surface ss using silk thread. See Working the stitches. For all remaining lines indicated in green, work with finer

vertical centre line

Silk Thread

Finer Thread

1sq = 10cm

124

thread. Remove embroidery from frame and secure all loose ends firmly on the wrong side. Repeat for the remaining three sections. Gently blow away any surplus tailor's chalk.

Edging
Surface ss over the tacks marking the circle. Using small sharp-pointed scissors, cut away the surrounding net close to the stitching.

To make up
Press the veil carefully over a dry cloth with a cool iron. Avoid over-pressing so as not to flatten the work. Do not pull the edge out of shape.

Working the stitches

Attaching the thread

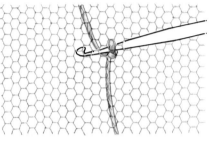

Make a slip loop on the hook. Remove the hook and, with RS facing, insert into the net. Replace the slip loop on the hook and draw it through to the right side.

Surface slip stitch

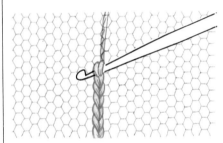

1 Attach the yarn. Holding the slip knot at the back of the work, *insert the hook into the next hole. Wind the yarn round the hook and draw through the loop on the hook. Repeat from * to end.

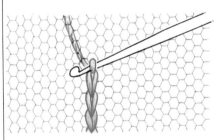

2 Inserting the hook into every hole forms very small stitches. Work longer stitches by inserting the hook into every second or third hole, extending the yarn over the net.

Couching
Yarn that is too thick to pass through the net can be couched with surface slip stitch using a matching fine yarn.

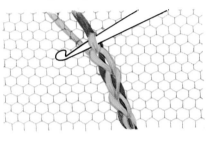

Attach the fine yarn to the net just to the right of the design line. Place the heavy yarn on to the design line. *Holding the latter in place, insert the hook into the net just to the left of the design line and work a slip stitch with the fine yarn. Insert the hook just to the right of the design line and work a slip stitch. Repeat from *, working long stitches.

Beaded slip stitch

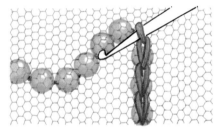

Thread beads on to the yarn before you begin. With the *wrong* side facing, attach the yarn and anchor with a short slip stitch. *Bring the first bead up close to the work and insert the hook into the net just beyond the bead. Wind the yarn round the hook and work one slip stitch. Work from * to end.

Fastening off

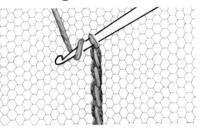

After working the last stitch, remove the hook from the loop. Insert the hook from back to front into the net, replace the loop and draw it through to the back of the work. Cut off the yarn, wind the yarn round the hook and draw through the end of yarn. Pull yarn to secure.

Extended double crochet
Double crochet can be used to outline a shape or as an edging. First outline the shape with slip stitch, inserting the hook into every alternate hole.

1 Attach the yarn three to eight holes outside the outline. Anchor the yarn with a short slip stitch. Extending the loop on the hook, insert the hook into a slipstitch of the outline. Yarn round hook and draw through the loop on the hook.

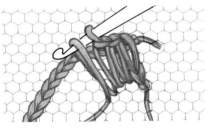

2 Insert the hook into the net as before and draw up the yarn to the outline. Insert the hook into the next slip stitch, yarn round hook and draw through both loops on the hook. Work from * to end.

Irish crochet patterns

**For those who love Irish crochet: a pretty T-shirt for a small girl
and, for you, an heirloom waistcoat.**

Materials

Elaborate Irish crochet fabrics, formed from a rich combination of flowers, leaves and shamrocks together with picot mesh, and traditionally worked in fine cotton, are amongst the most beautiful of all crochet laces.

Although other, thicker yarns are sometimes used, Irish crochet looks best when worked in fine cotton like the number 5 cotton used to make the T-shirt and waistcoat given here. If you have never worked with fine cotton before, you may meet tension problems. In this case, you will find it helpful to work sample motifs first.

Traditional Irish crochet as in the basic waistcoat is in the heirloom class

— similar pieces made in the last century are now much sought after — so look after it carefully. Wash gently in mild soapflakes, shape it on a towel and allow it to dry naturally.

Child's T-shirt

Sizes
To fit 58 [61:64]cm chest
Length 35 [38:41]cm
Sleeve seam 9cm
Note Instructions for larger sizes are given in square brackets []; where there is only one set of figures it applies to all sizes.

Tension
8 loops and 17 rows to 10cm over mesh pattern

Abbreviations
See page 101

You will need
For child's T-shirt, see sizes, above

4 [4:5] × 25g balls of Twilley's Lyscordet
2.50mm crochet hook
1 small button

Back
Using 2.50mm hook make 79 [82:85] ch.
Base row 1dc into 7th ch from hook, *4ch, miss next 2ch, 1dc into next ch, rep from * to end. Turn. 25 [26:27] 4ch loops.
Patt row 6ch, *1dc into next 4ch loop, 4ch, rep from * to last loop, 1dc into last loop. Turn.
Rep patt row until work measures 21 [23:25]cm from beg.
Shape armholes
Next row Ss across first 4ch loop and to centre of next loop, 1dc into centre of same loop, work 22 [23:24] loops. Turn.
Rep last row once more, working 20 [21:22] loops. Turn. **
Next row Ss across first 4ch loop and to centre of next loop, 1dc into centre of same loop, work 19 [20:21] loops. Turn.
Cont without further shaping until work measures 33 [36:39]cm from beg.
Shape shoulders
Next row Ss across first 2 4ch loops and to centre of next loop, 1dc into same loop, work 14 [15:16] loops. Turn.
Rep last row once more, working 10 [11:12] loops. Turn.

Next row Ss across first 4ch loop and to centre of next loop, 1dc into centre of same loop, work 8 [9:10] loops. Turn.
Next row Ss to centre of first 4ch loop, 1dc into same loop, work 7 [8:9] loops.
Fasten off.

Front
Work as given for back to **
Divide for neck
Next row Ss across first 4ch loop and to centre of next loop, 1dc into centre of same loop, work 9 [10:10] loops, turn.
Cont on these loops only without further shaping until work measures 31 [32:35]cm from beg, ending at neck edge.
Shape neck
Next row Ss across next 2 4ch loops, 1dc into next dc, 6ch, 1dc into first 4ch loop, patt to end. Turn. 7 [8:8] loops.
Patt one row without shaping.
Next row Ss to centre of first 4ch loop, 1dc into same loop, patt to end. Turn. 6 [7:7] loops.
Patt one row without shaping.
Rep last shaping row once more. 5 [6:6] loops.
Shape shoulder
Next row Ss across first 2 4ch loops and to centre of next loop, 1dc into same loop, patt to end. Turn. 2 [3:3] loops.
Next row 6ch, 1dc into first loop, 4ch, 1dc into next loop.
Fasten off.
Rejoin yarn to next 4ch loop at beg of neck division and work 2nd side of neck to correspond with first, reversing all shaping.

Sleeves (both alike)
Using 2.50mm hook, make 52 [55:58] ch.
Base row As for Back. 16 [17:18] loops.
Continue in patt as for Back until work measures 9cm from beg.
Shape top
Next row Ss across first 4ch loop and to centre of next loop, 1dc into same loop, patt across 13 [14:15] loops. Turn.
Next row Ss to centre of first 4ch loop, 1dc into same loop, patt across 12 [13:14] loops. Turn.
Patt 2 rows without shaping.
Next row Ss to centre of first 4ch loop, 1dc into same loop, patt across 11 [12:13] loops. Turn.

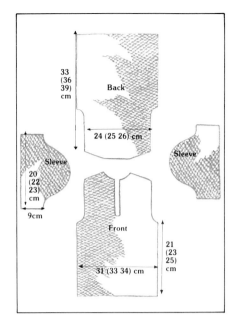

Next row Ss to centre of first 4ch loop, 1dc into same loop, patt across 10 [11:12] loops. Turn.
Rep last 4 rows, work one loop less on each dec row until 8 [9:10] loops rem.
Rep last 2 rows only until 4 [5:6] loops rem.
Fasten off.

To make up
Join shoulder seams. Set in sleeves. Join side and sleeve seams, using an invisible seam (see page 129).
Lower edging
Using 2.50mm hook and with RS facing, join yarn to a side seam, 1ch, * 2dc into first loop, 3ch, ss to first of 3ch — picot formed —, 3dc into next loop, picot, rep from * all round lower edge, ending with ss to first ch.
Fasten off.
Neck edging
Using 2.50mm hook and with RS facing, join yarn to a shoulder seam and work as for Lower edging.
Sleeve edgings
Using 2.50mm hook and with RS facing, join yarn to sleeve seam and work as for Lower edging.

Rosebud (see Working raised motifs)
Using 2.50mm hook, make 6ch, join with a ss to form a circle.
1st round 6ch, (1tr, 3ch) 5 times into circle, ss into 3rd of 6th ch.
2nd round (1dc, 1htr, 3tr, 1htr, 1dc) into each 3ch loop.
3rd round Working behind last round, 1dc round first tr on 1st round, *5ch, 1dc round next tr on

1st round, rep from * ending with ss into first dc.

4th round (1dc, 1htr, 5tr, 1htr, 1dc) into each 5ch loop, ss to first dc. Fasten off. work 3 more rosebuds in the same way.

Leaf

Using 2.50m hook, make 16ch.
Base row 1dc into 3rd ch from hook, 1dc into each ch to last ch, 3dc into last ch, 1dc into each ch along opposite side of foundation ch, 1dc into turning ch.
On following rows work into *back* loop only of each st:
1st row 1dc into each of next 11dc. Turn.
2nd row 1ch, miss first st, 1dc into each of next 10dc (1dc, 1ch, 1dc) into centre dc, 1dc into each dc to within 4dc of tip of leaf, turn.
3rd row 1ch, miss first dc, 1dc into each dc to 1ch at base of leaf, (1dc, 1ch, 1dc) into 1ch sp, 1dc into each dc to within 3dc of previous row.
4th and 5th rows As 3rd.
6th row As 3rd, working 3dc into 1ch sp at base of leaf.
Fasten off. Work 5 more leaves in the same way.

To make up

Sew motifs around neck as shown. Sew on button. Using 2.50mm hook, work 6ch. Fasten off. Sew loop to neck to correspond with button.

Traditional Irish waistcoat

Note Before beginning, see Traditional waistcoat pattern. Because of the method of working, it is not possible to give exact yarn quantity, size and tension.

Abbreviations

See page 101

You will need

For the waistcoat
Twilley's Lyscordet as required (waistcoat shown was made from eight 25g balls)
2.50mm crochet hook
Paper dressmaking pattern for simple waistcoat
Medium-weight interfacing as required

Rose (see working raised motifs)

Using 2.50mm hook, make 8ch, join with a ss to form a circle.
1st round 6ch, (1tr, 3ch) 7 times into circle, ss to 3rd of 6ch.

2nd round (1dc, 1htr, 3tr, 1htr, 1dc) into each 3ch loop.
3rd round Working behind last round, 1dc round first tr on 1st round, (5ch, 1dc round next tr) 7 times, 5ch, ss to first dc.
4th round (1dc, 1htr, 5tr, 1htr, 1dc) into each 5ch loop.
5th round Working behind last round, 1dc round first dc of 3rd round, (7ch, 1dc round next dc) 7 times, 7ch, ss to first dc.
6th round (1 dc, 1htr, 7tr, 1htr, 1dc) into each 7ch loop.
7th round Working behind last round, 1dc round first dc of 5th round, (9ch, 1dc round next dc) 7 times, 9ch, ss to first dc.
8th round (1dc, 1htr, 9tr, 1htr, 1dc) into each 9ch loop, ss to first dc. Fasten off. Make one more rose in the same way.

Rosebud

Work as for child's T-shirt. Make 21.

Leaf

Work as for child's T-shirt. Make 22.

To make up (see Traditional waistcoat pattern)
Cut out back and fronts of waistcoat from interfacing, omitting seam allowances round neck, armholes and front and lower edges. Join side seams.
Tack motifs into position on to interfacing as shown.
Using 2.50mm hook, join yarn to first motif and work picot mesh as follows:
Base row *2ch, 1 picot (3ch, ss into first of 3ch), 3ch, 1 picot, 2ch, ss into next motif or same motif, rep from * to end. Turn.
Patt row 2ch or ss along a motif as necessary, *1 picot, 3ch, rep from * to end.
Continue filling in between motifs, working straight rows of picot mesh across back. When all motifs are joined and interfacing covered with picot mesh, remove all tacking. Join shoulder seams.

Edging

Working over a cord of 3 strands of Lyscordet, *(3dc, 1 picot) into each ch loop all round neck, front and lower edges and round armholes.

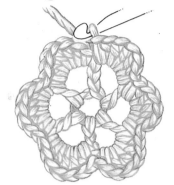

Working raised motifs

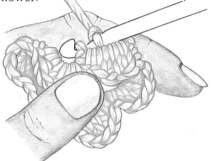

1 The outer petals of the flowers on the T-shirt and waistcoat are worked behind the previous rounds to give a three-dimensional appearance. Work the first two rounds as given in the pattern to form a small flower.

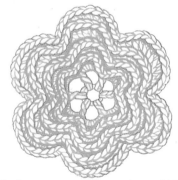

2 Holding the work as shown and inserting the hook from back to front, work one double crochet round the stem of the next treble on the first round. Work five chain. Continue in this way, ending with a slipstitch to the first double crochet. On the next round work in the chain loops to form the petals.

3 To form a many-layered motif like the rose on the waistcoat, repeat step 2, working the double crochet round the corresponding double crochet on the last-but-one round. Make petals larger by working more chain and then more graduated stitches on the following round.

Working over a cord

To give a raised effect, Irish motifs — which are usually worked in double crochet — may be worked over a cord. Use as a cord either three or four strands of cotton twisted together or a thicker cotton in the same colour. When the motif is completed, cut off the cord close to the stitches.

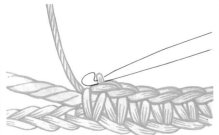

1 Having worked the foundation chain, hold the cord at the back of the work in the left hand. Work into the chain and over the cord at the same time.

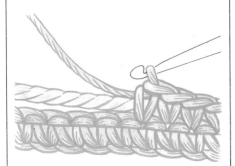

2 At the end of the row, turn and work the next row over the cord, holding the cord at the back of the work.

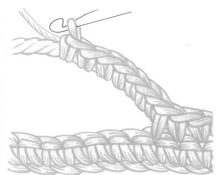

3 To work over the cord alone, hold it away from the main body of the crochet, and work along the cord, pushing the stitches together to cover the cord.

Traditional waistcoat pattern

For the basic outline, choose a fairly simple dressmaking pattern without elaborate shaping. Make up the pattern using a medium-weight interfacing (you could use the traditional muslin or linen), omitting shoulder seams and cutting away seam or hem allowances on the front, neck and lower edges. Ignore facings and do not seam or set in sleeves.

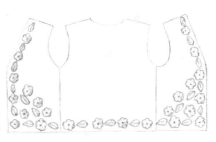

1 Lay the seamed pattern pieces out flat and arrange the motifs on the interfacing as you wish. Pin and tack the motifs firmly to the interfacing.

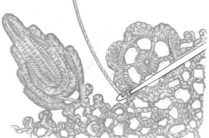

2 Using a matching yarn, fill in the spaces between the pattern motifs with picot mesh. Join the mesh to the edge of the motifs as you work using double crochet or slip stitch. Do not worry if the mesh seems irregular. This is unavoidable and adds to the beauty of the lace.

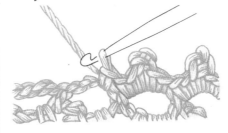

3 Remove the work from the interfacing and, after blocking, seam shoulder and sleeve seams and set in sleeves (see below). Work a narrow picot edging into the neck, front and lower edges, or work a separate edging and sew it to the mesh.

Seaming lace fabrics

Do not press Irish or any other crochet lace, but pin out the work to the correct size and lightly damp it. Allow it to dry naturally.

1 With right sides upwards, place the pieces edge to edge as shown. Secure a matching thread to the lower corner of the RH piece.

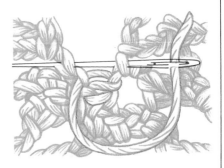

2 Insert the needle under one thread on the left-hand edge, insert the needle under one thread on the right-hand edge. Continue in this way, pulling the thread tightly so that the seam is invisible, but not so tightly that the work puckers.

Chapter 6

Filet Crochet

Filet crochet is instantly recognizable by the way in which designs are built up from solid blocks (trebles) worked on an even mesh background. It produces a firm, smooth-textured fabric traditionally used for curtains, bedspreads and many other home furnishings, where it is possible to create the most beautiful pictorial designs on a large scale.

Of all the so-called imitation laces (knitting and crochet fall into this category), it is the easiest to work — usually from a charted diagram, although the first two or three lines of a pattern are frequently written, and thereafter reference is made to the corresponding chart.

If you have never crocheted before, filet crochet is the perfect starting point. You'll be amazed how easy it is, and how quickly you can produce tasteful edgings and garments, pretty bedroom curtains, beautiful bedspreads and a host of other lacy items — all of which would make very acceptable gifts for you and your friends and family.

Filet sun top

Fine cotton has been used to make a pretty filet crochet summer top, patterned with roses and bordered with simple filet lace.

Materials

Filet crochet is derived from two basic stitches — treble and chain stitch. Motifs are created against a trellis of chain stitch and single trebles by building up blocks of trebles. Cottons of varying thicknesses are most frequently used as these give a firmer shape than other softer yarns. Very fine, light-weight cottons worked on a fine hook can be used to make lacy edgings and insertions which can be added to household linens such as tablecloths, handkerchiefs, napkins, whereas thicker threads are suitable for making summer tops and shawls.

Traditionally filet crochet was worked in white or écru cotton, but these cottons are now available in many different colours. Thicker knitting yarns are sometimes used, but the most effective results are achieved by using crisp cottons so that the motifs stand out clearly against the background net.

Tension

20 spaces and 20 rows to 10cm on 1.25mm crochet hook

Abbreviations

See page 101

You will need

For a sun top, to fit 86-91 [91-96]cm bust 35cm in length excluding straps

Note Instructions for larger sizes are in square brackets []; where there is one set of figures it applies to all sizes.

Seven 20g balls Coats Chain Mercer Crochet Cotton No. 20
1.25mm crochet hook
5 buttons

Top (both sizes) (see Working filet crochet)
Using 1.25mm hook make 207 ch.
1st row 1tr into 4th ch from hook, 1tr into each of next 2ch, (2ch, miss 2ch, 1tr into next ch) twice, (2 sps made), 1tr into each of next 3ch (block made), now work 60 sps, 1 block, 2 sps, 1 block. Turn.
2nd row 3ch, miss first tr, 1tr into each of next 3tr (block made over block at beg of row), (2ch, 1tr into next tr) twice, (2 sps made over 2 sps), 1tr into each of next 3tr (block made over block) now work 47 sps, (2tr into next sp, 1tr into next tr) twice, (2 blocks made over 2 spaces) now work 11 sps, 1 blk, 2 sps, 1tr into each of next 2tr, 1tr into next ch (block made over block at end of row). Turn.
3rd row 1ss into each of first 4tr (1 block dec) 3ch, (2tr into next sp, 1tr into next tr) twice, 2ch, miss 2tr, 1tr into next tr (sp made over block), now work 10 sps, 1 block, 2 spaces, 1 block, 23 spaces, 2 blocks, 22 spaces, 2 blocks. Turn.
4th row 5ch, 1tr into 4th ch from hook, 1tr into next ch, 1tr into next tr, (block inc at beg of row) 2 spaces, 1 block, 20 sps, 1 block, 2 spaces, 1 block, 22 sps, 1 block, 2 sps, 1 block, 10 sps, 1 block, 1 sp, 2 ch, miss 2tr, insert hook into next ch and draw yarn through, yrh and draw through one loop on hook (a foundation ch made), complete as a tr, *yrh, insert hook into foundation ch and draw yarn through, yrh and draw through one loop on hook (another foundation ch made) complete as a tr, rep from * twice more (a block inc at end of row), 3ch. Turn.

1st size only
5th-88th rows Work from Chart, noting that 88th row is marked by arrow.
Turn chart and work from 88th row marked by arrow back to first row. Fasten off.
2nd size only
5th-94th rows Work from chart, noting that 94th row is marked by an asterisk.
Turn chart and work from 94th row marked by * back to first row. Fasten off.

Buttonhole band (both sizes)
1st row Join yarn to 3rd tr made on last row, 1dc into same place as join, (2dc into next sp, 1dc into next tr) twice, 1dc into each of next 3tr, (2dc into next sp, 1dc into next tr) 60 times, 1dc into each of next 3tr (2dc into next sp, 1dc into next tr) twice, 1ch. Turn.
2nd row 1dc into each of first 58 dc, (5ch, miss 5dc, 1dc into each of next 28dc) 4 times, 5ch, miss 5dc, 1dc into each of next 4dc, 1ch. Turn.
3rd row (1dc into each dc, 5dc into next 5ch sp) 5 times, 1dc into each dc, 5ch. Turn.
4th row Miss first 3dc, 1tr into next dc, (2ch, miss 2dc, 1tr into next dc) 65 times. Fasten off.

Button band (both sizes)
1st row Join yarn to 3rd tr made on first row, 1dc into same place as join, (2dc into next sp, 1dc into base of next tr) twice, 1dc into base of each of next 3tr, (2dc into next sp, 1dc into base of next tr) 60 times, 1dc into base of each of next 3tr, (2dc into next sp, 1dc into base of next tr) twice, 1ch. Turn.
2nd row 1dc into each dc, 1ch. Turn.
3rd row 1dc into each dc, 5ch. Turn.
4th row As 4th row of buttonhole band.

Shoulder straps (make 2)
Using 1.25mm hook make 9ch.
1st row 2 blocks. Turn.
2nd row 5ch, inc 1 block, 2 sps, 1 inc block. Turn.
3rd row 3ch, 1 block, 2 sps, 1 block. Turn.
4th row Dec 1 block, 3ch, 2 blocks, Turn.
Rep 2nd to 4th rows until work measures 37cm from beg, or length required.
Fasten off.

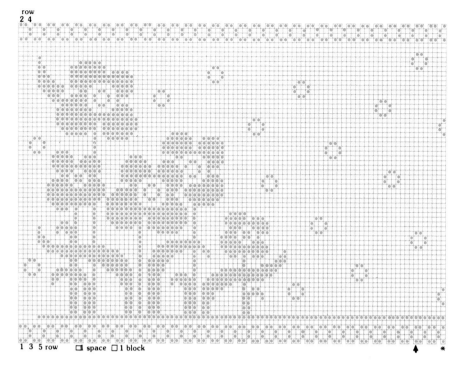

row
2 4

1 3 5 row   □ space □ 1 block

To make up
Sew shoulder straps in place. Sew on buttons to correspond with buttonholes.

Cord (make 2)
(see Making a crochet cord)
Commence with 2ch, holding this between finger and thumb of left hand, work 1dc into 2nd ch from hook, turn, inserting hook into back of loop, work 1dc into foundation loop of 2nd ch made, *turn, insert hook into 2 loops at side, yarn over and draw through 2 loops on hook, yarn over and draw through rem 2 loops, rep from * until work measures 120cm from beg, or length required. Fasten off. Slot cords through at waistline and top.
Damp and pin out to measurements. Leave to dry.

Working filet crochet

Filet charts

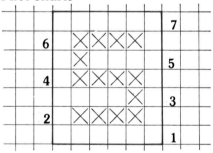

1 Filet crochet is usually worked by following graphed charts, in which *blocks* of treble and chain *spaces* are shown as crosses and blank squares respectively. In the chart above, each blank square represents a two-chain space plus a conecting treble, while each cross represents two treble plus a connecting treble.

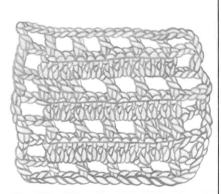

2 The sample above has been worked following the chart in step 1 Read the odd-numbered rows from right to left and the even-numbered rows from left to right.

Filet crochet

Mesh background

1 Make a multiple of three chain plus two extra. Work one treble into the eighth chain from the hook. *Make two chain. Miss the next two foundation chain and work one treble into the next foundation chain. Continue from * to the last foundation chain.

2 On following rows begin by working five chain to count as the first treble and two-chain space. Work one treble into the next treble. *Work two chain and then one treble into the next treble. Continue from * to the end, working the last treble into the turning chain.

Beginning with a block

1 To begin a piece of filet with a block of treble, make enough foundation chain for the spaces and blocks on the first row. Work two more chain and then work one treble into the fourth chain from the hook; the first three chain count as the first treble. Complete the first block by working one treble into each of the next two foundation chain.

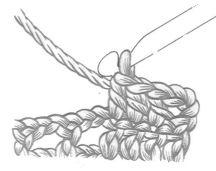

2 On following rows, to begin with a block work three chain to count as the first treble. Miss the first treble and work one treble into each of the next three treble.

Working a block above a space

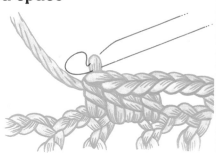

Work one treble into the next connecting treble. Then work two treble into the space, followed by one treble into the next connecting treble.

Working a space above a block

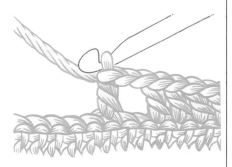

Work one treble into the next connecting treble. Work two chain, miss the next two treble and work one treble into the next treble.

Making a crochet cord

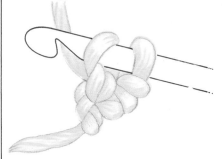

1 Start with 2ch. Hold the chain between finger and thumb of left hand and work 1dc into 2nd ch from hook. Turn the work so that the foundation ch is at the top. Insert hook into back loop and work 1dc into foundation loop of 2nd ch made at beginning.

2 Turn chain so that bottom is now at top next to hook and insert hook into 2 loops which are at side of chain.

3 Take yarn over and through 2 loops on hook. Yarn over hook and through remaining 2 loops to make a twisted stitch. By turning stitches in this way you achieve a twisted cord.

Sheet trims

For an individual touch, sew a long strip of white filet, which says 'Sleep well' in three languages, on to a sheet.

Before you begin

Filet crochet, with its square blocks and spaces, lends itself particularly well to monograms. Two alphabets in contrasting styles are given here, but it is quite a simple matter to graph your own.

Materials

Monograms or complete words and phrases worked in filet crochet take some time to make, so take care that the letters can be clearly seen. Use a fairly fine, untextured yarn like the number 20 cotton used to make the sheet trim shown here. Make sure that the colour of the trim contrasts strongly with that of the sheets — similar colours would make the monograms illegible. Always remove the trim before washing the sheet.

Tension

10½ spaces and 11 rows to 5cm worked over plain filet mesh

Abbreviations

See page 101

You will need

For trim to fit a single [double] sheet 14cm wide with a total length of 180 [230]cm. Length of lettered panel 90 [126]cm.
Note Instructions for the larger size are in square brackets []; where there is only one set of figures, it applies to both sizes.

5[7] × 20g balls of Coats Chain Mercer Crochet Cotton No. 20
1.25mm crochet hook

Single-sheet trim

Using 1.25m hook, make 83ch.
Base row 1tr into 8th ch from hook, (2ch, miss next 2ch, 1tr into next ch) 4 times, 1tr into each of next 6ch, (2ch, miss next 2ch, 1tr into next ch) 19 times. Turn.
1st row (WS) 5ch, miss first tr, (1tr into next tr, 2ch) 17 times, 1tr into next tr, 2tr into next sp, 1tr into next tr, (2ch, miss next 2tr, 1tr into next tr) twice, 2tr into next sp, 1tr into

next tr, (2ch, 1tr into next tr) 3 times, 2ch, 1tr into last sp. Turn.
Last row forms 18 sps, 1 block, 2 sps, 1 block, 4 sps.
2nd row 5 sps, 2 blocks, 19 sps. Turn.
3rd row 18 sps, 1 block, 2 sps, 1 block 4 sps. Turn.
Rep 1st and 2nd rows until a total of 90 rows have been worked from beg. Then work 180 rows of chart, beg 1st row at edge marked with an arrow. Work 90 rows to match those worked at beg of trim, ending with a WS row. Turn and do not fasten off.

Picot edging
(3dc, 3ch, ss to top of last dc — picot formed) into each sp to end.
Fasten off.

Double-crochet edging
With RS facing, rejoin yarn to first sp on opposite edge of trim, work 3dc into each sp to end. Fasten off.

Double-sheet trim
Work base and 1st-2nd rows as for single-sheet trim. Then rep 1st and 2nd rows until 104 rows have been worked from beg.
Work 252 rows of the chart, beg 1st row at the edge marked with an arrow. Work 104 rows to match those worked at beg of trim, ending with a WS row. Complete as for single.

To make up
Press work under a damp cloth. Sew trim to sheet (see Stab stitch, page 101), turn back as shown.

Graphing filet letters

You may prefer either to substitute the Roman lettering on the chart with letters from the Victorian alphabet given, or graph your own, as follows.

1 Using tracing paper and a soft pencil, trace the outline of the letter — it could be taken from a book, magazine or your own design. Turn over to the other side of the paper and carefully trace the outline of the letter as shown.

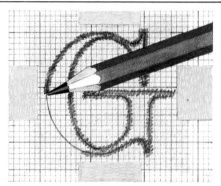

2 Turn back to the first side of the paper and stick the tracing to graph paper with masking tape to prevent slipping. Using a soft pencil, shade over the outline of the letter. The shape of the letter should appear on the graph paper.

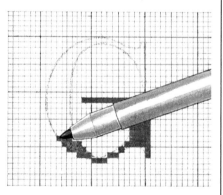

3 Remove the masking tape and tracing paper. Shade the squares of graph paper within the outline of the letter, shading squares which are partly outside to obtain a good shape. When working the filet, the shaded areas will be blocks and the clear areas will be mesh.

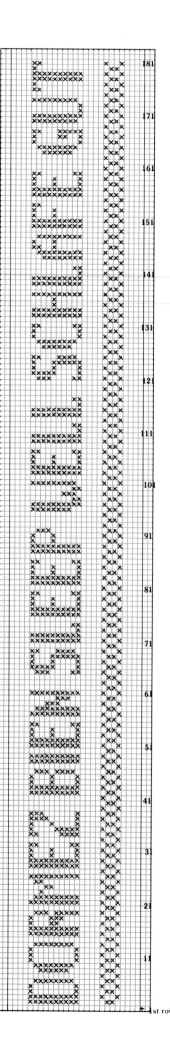

181
171
161
151
141
131
121
111
101
91
81
71
61
51
41
31
21
11
1st row

Chart for sheet trim

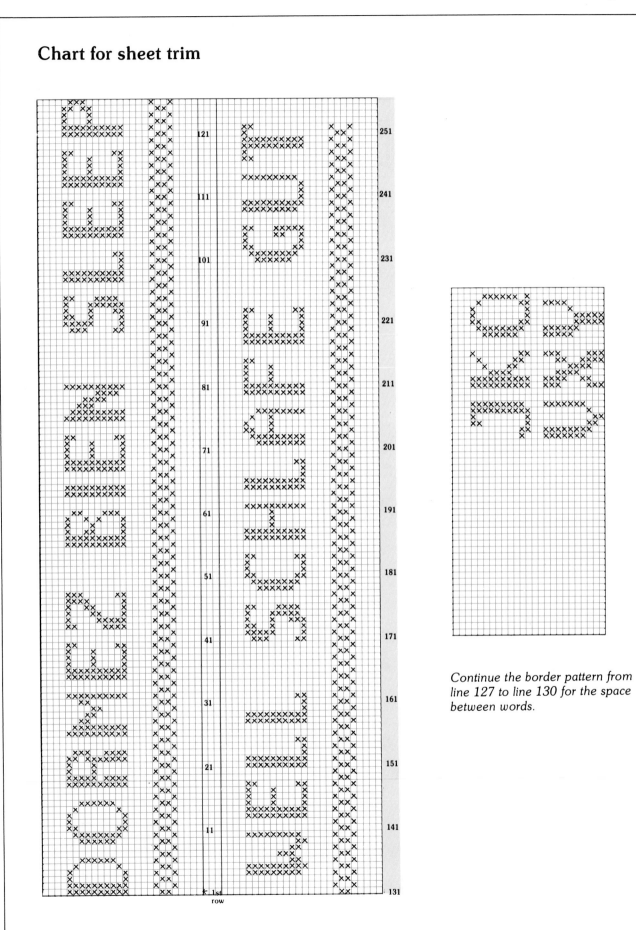

Continue the border pattern from line 127 to line 130 for the space between words.

Monogrammed handkerchiefs

Treat yourself or make someone else a highly personalized present by monogramming a handkerchief with a filet crochet corner trim. Use the Victorian alphabet as your guide.

Tension
26 sps and 30 rows to 10cm on 0.75mm crochet hook

Abbreviations
See page 101

You will need
For a corner trim, 15cm by 11cm by 11cm

One 20g ball Coats Mercer crochet cotton No. 60

1 handkerchief with narrow hem 0.75mm crochet hook

Crochet triangle
Using 0.75mm hook, make 7ch.
Base row (1tr, 2ch, 1dtr) into 7th ch from hook. Turn.
1st row 9ch, 1tr into dtr, 2ch, 1tr into next tr, 2ch, (1tr, 2ch, 1dtr) into last loop. Turn.
2nd row 6ch, 1tr in dtr, 2ch, (1tr into next tr, 2ch) 3 times, (1tr, 2ch, 1dtr) into last loop. Turn.
3rd row 6ch, 1tr into dtr, 2ch, (1tr into next tr, 2ch) 5 times, (1tr, 2ch, 1dtr) into last loop. Turn.
Increase in this way for three more rows or until there are sufficient 2ch sps across row to begin working initial from chart (see page 138). While working from chart cont to inc at row ends. After completing initial work

one further row, inc at ends. Fasten off.

To make up
Press crochet with a damp cloth. Tack in position on fabric at corner of handkerchief. Using matching crochet cotton, sew long edge of crochet to fabric, neatly catching each space with one or two tiny stitches. Fold back corner of fabric. Cut off excess, leaving 6mm for hem. Roll hem and catch down with matching sewing thread, to hide previous sewing.

Edging
Join crochet cotton to corner of crochet and work 4dc into each sp. Work dc evenly around hem, inserting hook into fabric. Join with ss to 1st dc. Fasten off. Press complete handkerchief with a damp cloth.

Filet mat and curtain

**Prettify a window with a delicate curtain that pictures
a row of curious cats beneath lacy drapes,
then repeat the theme in a matching mat.**

Materials

So that all details can be seen to their best advantage, even the simplest form of picture filet is best worked in smooth, fine cotton or linen threads. The resulting fabric holds its shape well both in use and even after frequent laundering.

Tension

16 sp and 16 rows to 10cm square

Abbreviations

See page 101

You will need

For a mat, 40cm by 25.5cm and a curtain, 70cm by 44cm

Mat

2 balls of Phildar Perlé No. 5

Curtain

4 balls of Phildar Perlé No. 5
One 2.50mm crochet hook

To make the mat

Commence with 125ch, 1tr into 4th ch from hook, 1tr into each tr to end.

123tr.
Next row 3ch, 1tr into each tr to end, turn.
Continue in pattern working from chart A.
Fasten off.

Finishing

Damp the crochet and pin it out to shape, aligning the edges. Leave to dry in an airy place. Press under a cloth, if required. Add crispness with a light coating of spray starch.

To make the curtain

Commence with 219ch, 1tr into 4th ch from hook, 1tr into each tr to end. 217ch.
Next row 3ch, 1tr into each tr to end. Continue in pattern working from chart B and level rows when centre of work is reached.
Fasten off.
Finish in the same way as for the mat.
For hanging, work a series of chain loops along the top edge to take a curtain wire or brass rod.

chart A (above); chart B (right)

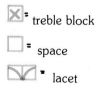

= treble block

= space

= lacet

Stars and moon curtain

Let in plenty of twinkling moonlight with this delightful half curtain
in filet net. Make it for a small child's room or as a foil for landing
or even bathroom windows.

Materials
Fine, cotton, linen or equivalent synthetic threads in white, natural or soft pastel colours, in plain or variegated tones, are ideal for working the curtain. All these threads launder well and will keep the curtain shape looking fresh and crisp. A pretty brass rod will add extra sparkle.

Tension
9 sps and 11 rows to 10cm on 2.50mm hook

Abbreviations
See page 101

You will need
For a curtain, 91cm by 60cm

Six 50g balls of Twilley's Stalite
2.50m crochet hook
Pole to hang curtain

Note Curtain is worked from side edge to side edge.

Curtain
Using 2.50mm hook, make 178 ch.
Base row 1tr into 8th ch from hook, 7ch, miss next 7ch, 1tr into next ch, (2ch, miss next 2ch, 1tr into next ch) 46 times. 1tr into each of next 21ch, 2ch, miss next 2ch, 1tr into last ch. Turn. 1 sp, 1 long sp, 46 sp, 7 blocks, 1 sp.
1st row 5ch, miss first tr, 1tr into next tr, 1tr into each of next 3tr, 2ch, miss next 2tr, 1tr into each of next 10tr, 2ch, miss next 2tr, 1tr into each of next 4tr, (2ch, 1tr into next tr) 46 times, 7ch, 1tr into next tr, 2ch, 1tr into last sp. Turn. 1 sp, 1 block, 1 sp, 3 blocks, 1 sp, 1 block, 46 sp, 1 long sp, 1 sp.
2nd row 5ch, miss first tr, 1tr into next tr, 7ch, 1tr into next tr, (2ch, 1tr into next tr) 25 times, 2tr into next 2ch sp, 1tr into next tr, (2ch, 1tr into next tr) 20 times, 1tr into each of next 3tr, 2tr into next 2ch space, 1tr into next tr, 2ch, miss 2tr, 1tr into each of next 4tr, 2ch, miss 2tr, 1tr into next tr, 2tr into 2ch sp, 1tr into each of next 4tr, 2ch, 1tr into last sp. turn. 1 sp, 1 long sp, 25 sp, 1 block, 20 sp, 2 blocks, 1 sp, 1 block, 1 sp, 2 blocks, 1 sp.
3rd row 1 sp, 1 block, 2 sps, 1 block, 2 sps, 1 block, 18 sps, 1 block, (1 sp, 1 block) twice, 23 sps, 1 long sp, 1 sp. Turn.
Cont working from chart, always adding the long sp and edge sp to form the top edging of the curtain (not shown on the chart).

To make up
Lay out the finished curtain and, using a damp cloth and a light coating of spray starch, if preferred, press it carefully. To hang, you can either thread a decorative curtain pole through the long spaces of the top edging, or simply hang the curtain from brass or wooden curtain rings threaded through the edge.

Curtain chart

Café curtain

**The strong and beautiful lines and flowing flower and plant patterns
of art nouveau design are captured forever in a filet crochet curtain.**

Size
64cm by 73cm excluding edging

Tension
20 sps and 20 rows to 10cm over filet mesh worked on 1.25mm crochet hook

You will need
Nine 20g balls of Coats Chain Mercer-Crochet Cotton No. 20
1.25mm crochet hook

To make the curtain
Using 1.25mm hook make 384ch.

Base row (RS) 1tr into 4th ch from hook, 1tr into each of next 5ch, — 2 blocks or blks made —, * (2ch, miss next 2ch, 1tr into next ch) 3 times — 3 sps made —, 1tr into each of next 9ch — another 3 blks made —, rep from * 19 times more, (2ch, miss next 2ch, 1tr into next ch) 3 times, 1tr into each of next 6ch. Turn.

1st row 5ch, miss first 3tr, 1tr into next tr — sp made over blk at beg of row —, 1tr into each of next 3tr, — blk made over blk —, 2tr into next sp, 1tr into next tr — blk made over sp —, 1tr into next tr — blk made over sp —, (1sp, 2 blks, 1 sp) 41 times. Turn.

2nd row 3ch, work 126 blks, 2tr into next sp, 1tr into 3rd of last 5ch, (blk made over sp at end of row). Turn.

3rd row 3ch, miss first tr, 1tr into each of next 3tr — blk made over blk at beg of row —, 1 blk, (3 sps, 3 blks) 20 times, 3 sps, 1 blk, 1tr into each of next 2tr, 1tr into 3rd of last 3ch — blk made over blk at end of row —. Turn.

4th-16th rows Follow chart, always working from left to right until the centre is reached, then omitting the last blk or sp on the chart (as this is the central one) work back to the left for the 2nd half of the curtain, thus working the pattern in reverse.

17th row Work 5 sps, 14 blks, 3 sps, 2 blks, (3ch, miss next 2 sts, 1dc into next tr, 3ch, miss next 2 sts, 1tr into next st) 3 times — 3 lacets made —, follow chart to end of row. Turn.

18th row 5ch, 6 sps, 7 blks, 2 sps, 3 blks, 2 sps, 2 blks, 5ch, miss next 5 sts, 1tr into next st — bar made —, (5ch, 1tr into next tr) 3 times — 3 bars made over 3 lacets —, 4 blks, follow chart to end of row. Turn.

19th row 5ch, 14 sps, 3 blks, 2 sps, 1 blk, 3 lacets, 2 sps, 5tr over next bar, 1tr into next tr — 2 blks made over bar —, 2 sps, foll chart to row end.

20th-46th row Follow chart.

47th row 17 sps, 2 blks, 1 sp, 1 blk, 2 sps, 2tr over next bar, 1tr into centre ch of same bar, 2ch, 1tr into next tr — blk and sp made over bar —, 1 sp, follow chart to end of row. Work 48th-155th rows from chart. Fasten off.

Edging

Using 1.25mm hook rejoin yarn to
the bottom right-hand corner, 1dc
into same place as join, *2dc into
next row-end, 1dc into next st*, rep
from * to.* along side edge working
last dc into 3rd of 5ch at corner,
24ch, ss into last dc (— a loop made
—), (2dc into next sp, 1dc into next
tr, 24ch, ss into last dc) 127 times,
rep form * to * along next side
working last dc into foundation ch at
corner, 2dc into same place as last
dc, 1dc into each of next 6 sts, 8ch,
count back over the last 8dc just
worked, ss into next dc, working into
the 8ch loop just made work (3dc,
3ch) 3 times and 3dc, ss into the last
of the 6dc worked just before the 8ch
— a scallop made —, 2dc into next
sp, 1dc into next st, (1dc, 3ch, and
1dc) into next sp, 1dc into next st,
2dc into next sp, (1dc into each of
next 10 sts, 8ch, count back over the
last 9dc just worked and complete
scallop as before, 2dc into next sp,
1dc into next st, (1dc, 3ch, and 1dc)
into next sp, 1dc into next st, 2dc
into next sp) 20 times, 1dc into each
of next 6 sts, 2dc into same place as
first dc, ss into first dc, 8ch, count
back over the last 7dc just worked
and complete scallop at before.
Fasten off.

To make up

Using rustless pins, pin out the curtain
to size, dampen and leave to dry. Coat
lightly with spray starch, if preferred.

140

130

120

110

100

90

80

70

60

50

47th row

40

30

20

17th row

10

4th row

1

Key
bar
lacet
block(blk)
space(sp)

commence ch here ➞

centre

Cotton bag

This useful bag worked in fresh white cotton with a pretty rose motif on each side is worked in a small filet mesh. All the pieces are crocheted together with shell edging.

Before you begin

The pattern given for the bag uses a small mesh fillet net, where one chain is worked between trebles. However, the overall size of the bag can easily be increased by working a larger mesh, crocheting two chain between each treble. In Making the basic net, see page 148, figures are given in brackets for working the larger mesh.

Tension

20 sts and 9 rows to 5cm over filet pattern

Abbreviations

See page 101

You will need

For a bag 30 × 38cm
Seven 20g balls of Coats Chain

Mercer Crochet cotton No. 20
1.75mm crochet hook
60cm No. 6 piping cord for handles

To make the bag
Working the first side

Start at centre of bottom gusset.
Make 112 ch.
Base row 1tr into 6th ch from hook,
* 1ch, miss 1ch, 1tr into next ch; rep

Read odd-numbered (right side) rows from right to left

Read even numbered (wrong side) rows from left to right

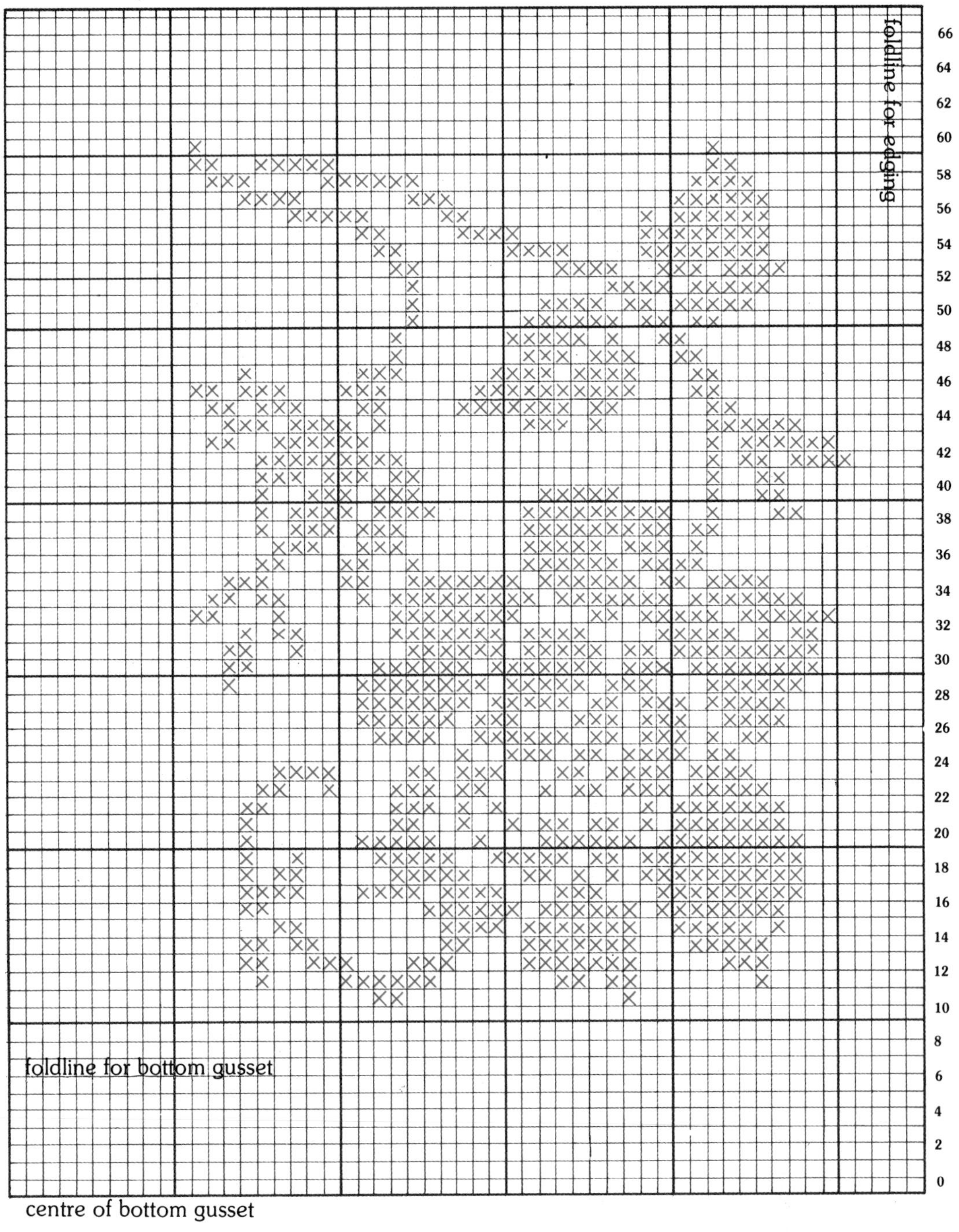

foldline for edging

foldline for bottom gusset

centre of bottom gusset

66 64 62 60 58 56 54 52 50 48 46 44 42 40 38 36 34 32 30 28 26 24 22 20 18 16 14 12 10 8 6 4 2 0

from * to end. 54 1ch sps.
1st row 4ch, 1tr into next tr, *1ch, 1tr into next tr; rep from * working last tr into 4th of 5ch.
2nd to 67th row Work from chart reading the rows as instructed.
Next row 1ch, 1dc into first tr, *1dc into next ch sp, 1dc into next tr; rep from * working last dc into 4th of 5ch.
Next row 1ch, 1dc into each dc to end. Repeat the last row 4 times more. Fasten off.

Working the second side
The second side of the bag is worked in the same way as the first side. With wrong side of work facing and working into other side of commencing ch, attach yarn to first ch, 4ch, miss first 2ch, 1tr into next ch, *1ch, miss 1ch, 1tr into next ch; rep from * to end. 54 1ch sps. Complete to match first side.

Side gussets
(Both alike) With wrong side facing attach yarn to top of 5th row as indicated on chart, 4ch, 1tr into top of next row end, * 1ch, 1tr onto top of next row end; rep from * 10 times more. 12 1ch sps. Work a further 61 rows in filet crochet, then work 6 rows in dc. Work other side to match.

Joining and edging sides
Place wrong sides together and work through both pieces thus: attach yarn to end of last dc row, 1dc in same place as join, miss 2 row ends (1htr, 2ch, 4tr = shell) into next row end, 1dc into sp at end of 67th row end, *1 shell into next row end, miss next row end, 1dc into next row end; rep from * to within corner sp, 1 shell into corner sp, now fold work along line as indicated and work through folded fabric, 1dc into next sp, ** 1 shell into next space, miss next space, 1dc into next sp; rep from ** to next corner, (1dc) into corner sp, now work through sps of main part and gusset thus: *1 shell into next row end, miss next row end, 1dc in next sp; rep from * 19 times, 1 shell into next sp, 1dc into next sp, 1 shell into next sp, miss next sp, miss 2 row ends, 1dc into next row end, 1 shell into next row end, miss 2 row ends, 1dc into last row end. Fasten off.

Making the handles
(Both alike) Cut cord in half. Make a length of ch 30cm long.
Base row 1dc into 2nd ch from hook 1dc into each ch to end.
1st row 1ch, 1dc in each dc to end. Rep last row until work is deep enough to fit around cord. Fasten off. Join crochet together over cord. Attach handles to wrong side 8cm from seam.

Making the basic net

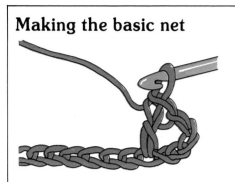

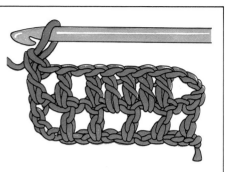

1 Make an even number of chain. Treble into 6th(8th) chain from hook — called one space. The 5(7) turning chain are counted as 3 chain for first treble, plus 1(2) chain for base and 1(2) chain for the top of the space.

4 Repeat step 3 on every row to make the basic mesh pattern, but working the last treble into the 3rd turning chain on subsequent rows each time.

3 Where 2 blocks are worked side by side, the blocks will consist of 5(7) treble. When counting stitches where blocks are worked together, remember that each extra block counts as 2(3) extra stitches since the centre treble joining blocks counts as the last treble of one block and the first treble of the next block.

Making the blocks

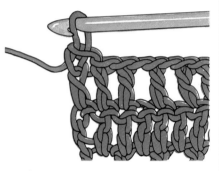

2 Miss next 1(2) chain, work a treble into next chain. Make 1(2) chain for next space, miss one chain, work 1 treble into next chain. 2 spaces made. Continue to work along chain to make the basic row of spaces.

1 Make one row of spaces following instructions for the basic net. Make 3 chain to count as the first treble of the next row. Work 1(2) treble into the first space of the previous row and then 1 treble into the next treble (or 1 treble into each of the next 2 trebles) adjacent to the space. First block consists of 3(5) trebles.

4 To work a space in the centre of several blocks, count trebles while working to make sure space is placed correctly. Here 2 spaces have been worked over 4 blocks consisting of 9 treble in all, missing 4th and 6th trebles and working 1 chain between trebles to create the 2 spaces.

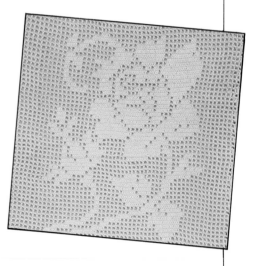

3 To build up mesh make 3 turning chain for first treble, plus 1(2) chain for first space. Work a treble into next treble of previous row, 1(2) chain, 1 treble into following treble. Continue working last treble into 4th turning chain.

2 Make a row of alternate blocks and spaces by working 1(2) chain, then 1 treble into next treble to make 1 space; 1(2) treble into next space and 1 treble into next treble for next block, across the row. Work last treble into 3rd turning chain.

Filet bedspread

This beautiful bedspread worked in fine cotton makes an heirloom
any family would be proud to own. Make either a single or double
bed size, and add a pretty border once it has been completed.

Before you begin

Deep lacy borders, which are such a feature of filet lace bedspreads and many other household items, may themselves be plain or decoratively shaped.

The edging can be worked lengthwise, so that the number of chain worked is equivalent to the length of the border, with the width determined by the number of rows worked. Or, it can be worked from side to side, so that the number of chain is equivalent to the width and the length is deter-

mined by the number of rows worked.

Either method can be used where a straight piece is required for edging pillowcases or sheets, but when making a border for a square or rectangle, use the second method, mitring the corners for a perfect fit.

Mitred corners

Filet patterns are usually shown in the form of a chart, with the blocks and spaces represented by symbols on squared paper. Edgings are shown in exactly the same way, with the corner

marked by drawing a line through the chart at an angle of 45°, so that the pattern is mirrored on each side of the line.

Note The pattern used in the steps (see Working mitred corners) consists of 4 treble worked for each block with three treble for each additional block, and two chain for each space.

Work the first side to the corner line, working one space or block less at the inner edge on every row until only one space or block remains. Turn the chart and work the other side of the corner

from the chart, but working an extra block or space at the inner edge to complete it.

It is a good idea to practise with simple patterns, using two colours, one for each side of the corner, so that you can see exactly how the mitred border is worked, before tackling the main project.

Tension
10 blocks/spaces and 14 rows to 10cm worked on 2.50mm hook

Note Each block consists of 4 treble, with 3 treble worked for each additional block where they are side by side, and 2 chain worked for each space.

Abbreviations
See page 101

You will need
For a bedspread, single 170cm by 230cm; double, 190cm by 230cm

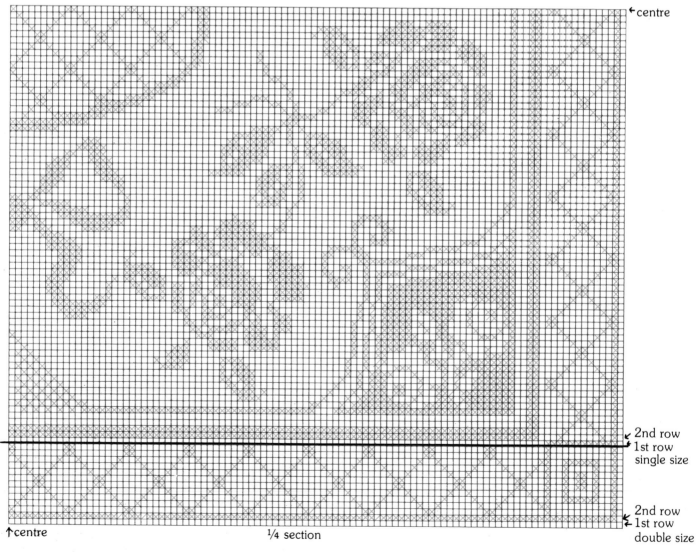

↑centre   ¼ section

←centre

↯ 2nd row
↯ 1st row
single size

↯ 2nd row
↯ 1st row
double size

Sixty 25g balls Twilleys Lyscordet
2.50mm crochet hook

To make bedspread
Commence with 617ch.
Single bedspread
1st row 1tr into 8th ch from hook,
1tr into each of next 36ch (2ch, miss
2ch, 1tr into next ch) 178 times, 1tr
into each of next 36ch, 2ch, miss
2ch, 1tr into last ch.
Double bedspread
1st row 1tr into 8th ch from hook,
*2ch, miss 2ch, 1tr into next ch, rep
from * to end.
Both sizes
Beginning from the 2nd row as
indicated cont in patt from chart,
when centre of row is reached, work
back in reverse to beg of row.
Continue until half of the bedspread
has been worked, then turn the chart
upside down and work the second
half.

To make borders
Single bed
Commence with 101ch, 1tr into 8th
ch from hook, 1tr into each of next
3ch (2ch, miss 2ch, 1tr into next ch)
3 times 1tr into each of next 3ch,
(2ch, miss 2ch, 1tr into next ch) 4
times, 1tr into each of next 3ch (2ch,
miss 2ch, 1tr into next ch) twice, 1tr
into each of next 3ch, (2ch, miss
2ch, 1tr into next ch) 15 times, 1tr
into each of last 9tr, turn.
Cont working in pattern from chart
until long enough to reach down side
edge of bedspread, turn corner as
given in graph, then work patt to go
along lower edge, turn 2nd corner
then work 2nd side to match first.
Double bed
Commence with 84ch, 1tr into 4th ch
from hook, 1tr into each of next 2ch
(2ch, miss 2ch, 1tr into next ch), 8
times, 1tr into each of next 6tr, (2ch,
miss 2ch, 1tr into next tr) 13 times,
1tr into each of next 9tr, turn.
Cont as given for single size, working
down side edge, along lower edge,
then up other side.

To make up
Press borders and bedspread. Here,
when working with large items, a
clean, well-padded floor space is
most useful. Pin out the separate
pieces to shape keeping them flat.
Using toning thread, stitch borders in
place matching blocks and spaces.
A light coating of spray starch adds a
fresh, crisp look.

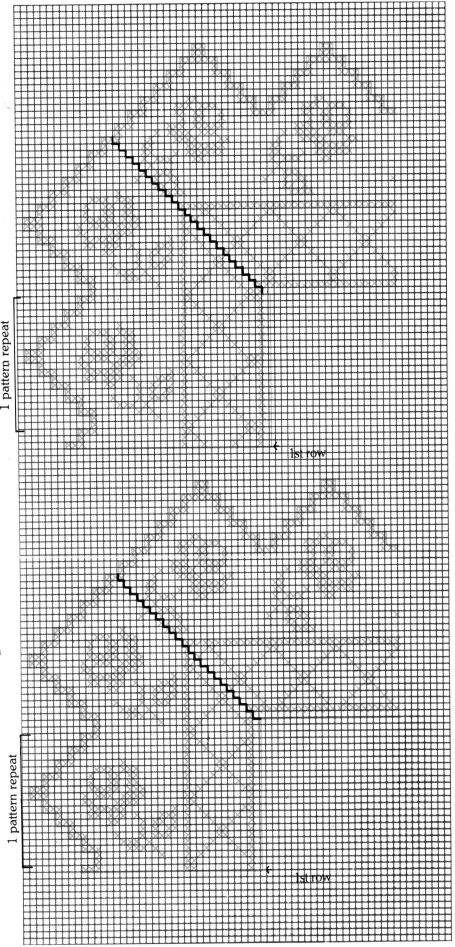

Working mitred corners

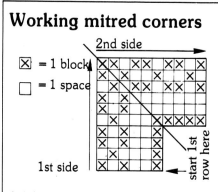

☒ = 1 block
☐ = 1 space

2nd side

1st side

start 1st row here

1 A line is drawn at an angle of 45° through the corner. Work edging from lower edge to corner, then turn chart and continue along second side to complete it.

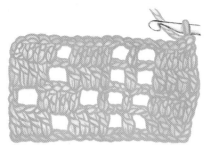

2 Make 21 chain. 1tr into 4th ch from hook, 1tr into each of next 2ch (first block), 2ch, miss 2ch, 1tr into next ch (first space). Complete first 4 rows from chart, ending at inner edge.

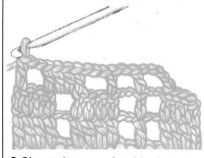

3 Slipstitch across first block and into last tr of block to decrease it. 5ch to count as first tr and 2ch space of next space. Continue in the pattern to the end of the row.

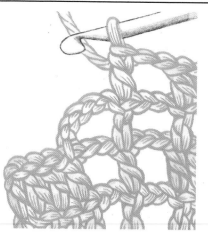

4 Turn. Work in patt from chart to end of row, leaving last space unworked to decrease a space at same (inner) edge.

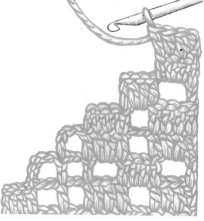

5 Continue to either slipstitch across a block or space at beginning of row, or miss a block or space at end of row, until 1 block remains. Work 1 more row on this block.

6 Turn crochet so that shaped edge is at top and you are ready to work second half of corner. Two colours are used here for clarity, the first called a and the second b.

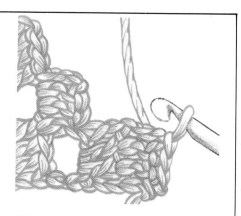

7 Where a pattern ends at outer edge after working last block or space, slipstitch across the end of this block or space so that you are in correct position to start second half of corner.

8 Turn chart to make it easier to read pattern. With b, 3ch to count as first tr, 2tr into side of block in a, 1tr in to top of second block in a to complete first block in b.

9 2ch, slipstitch into corner of next block in a. 5ch, slipstitch into corner of next block in a, making 2nd space.

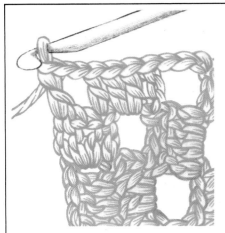

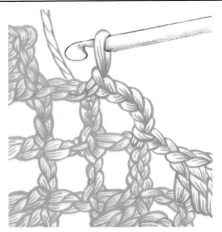

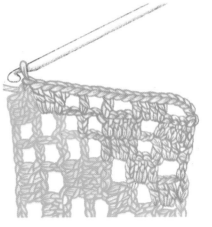

10 Turn. Slipstitch across first 2 chain just made and into 3rd chain. 2tr into next space. 1tr into next tr, 2ch, 1tr into top of turning chain.

12 5ch, slipstitch into 3rd of 5ch of next space in a to make next space. By working backwards and forwards in this way, the depth and shape of corner is maintained.

14 Work in patt from chart across stitches in b, then work 1 block into last space in a. Slip stitch to corner of next block in a to complete 2nd half.

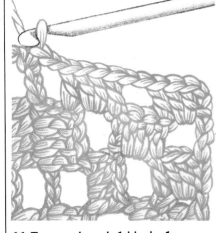

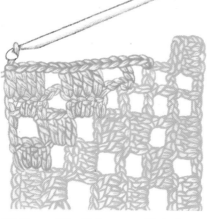

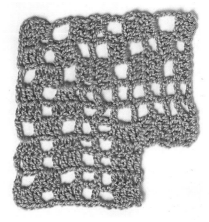

11 Turn and work 1 block, 1 space and 1 block over blocks and spaces of previous row. 2ch, slipstitch into corner of next space in a.

13 Turn. Slipstitch across 2 chain and into 3rd chain just made. 2ch, 1tr into next tr in b. Work 1 block, 1 space, and 1 block to end of row.

Once the corner has been completed, continue in pattern until the edging is the length required, or another corner is to be made.

Index

Suppliers

Sebalace, 76 Main Street, Addingham, Ilkley, West Yorkshire, LS29 0PL	Brussels tape and general lace, and tatting requisites
D. J. Hornsby, 149 High Street, Burton Latimer, Kettering, Northants.	General lace making requisites
Cavcrafts, 11 Fitzwilliam Avenue, Wath Upon Dearne, Rotherham, South Yorkshire S63 7HN	Wide variety of wooden bobbins
Bill Tuffnell, 2 Sylvester Lane, Beverley, East Yorkshire	Wide variety of glass bobbins and glass beads
C. & D. Sprignett, 21 Hillmorton Road, Rugby, Warwickshire	Reproduction bobbins in wood and bone, and handmade tatting shuttles
Mace and Nairn 89 Crane Street, Salisbury, Wiltshire	All lace threads, beeswax, lace scissors, linen lawn, pins
Mrs A. Sells, Lane Cover, 49 Pedley Lane, Clifton, Shefford, Bedfordshire	Acetate film, all lace threads, ballpoint needles, beeswax, finger shields, glazed cotton, lace scissors, linen lawn, muslin, net, pins, silver thimbles and tambour hooks

Useful Addresses

The Lace Guild,
The Hollies,
53 Audnam,
Stourbridge,
West Midlands DY8 4AE

Ring of Tatters,
Mrs. K. Conway,
'Myhalh',
1 Carr Street,
Birstall,
Batley,
West Yorkshire WF17 9DY

Knitting and Crochet Guild,
Mavis Walker (Editor),
63 Wheatlands,
Heston,
Hounslow,
Middlesex TW5 0S9

The Crochet Guild,
Miss L. Richardson,
Pool Foot,
Ambleside,
Cumbria LA22 9NE

The Guild of Needle laces
Kay Anderson,
4 Romsey Road,
Horndean,
Portsmouth,
Hants PO8 0EA